Mind Games

The twisted world of Brandon Omar Edwards vol.2

By: Eugene B. Oliver-Roberts

I would like to dedicate this book 2 my first 2 born niece and nephew
Torishiara M. Green & Brandon M. Oliver.
I luv u guys so much & I'm proud of you. Congratulation on your graduation the class of
2014. All my luv u from the bottom of my heart.
Your Uncle Brian. OXOX

Chapter One

I was standing behind one of my down to earth best friends which I never told April and Dashawn about and her name is Asia Grey. The secret I keep on a regular day to day basis. As I tried my best to help her fix her captivating gown while she stare at herself in the mirror with a priceless smile on her face. "I can't believe your getting married. I thought it would've been a few years ago though but like the old saying better late than never." I murmured wearing a smile. "I remember Khalid and my wedding nine years and half ago. The blessing god have given him and I don't deserve it at all." Okay I can't believe I just said that bullshit aloud true is I believe in god but after what I done back in Savannah Georgia let just say if you knew me back then your think of me in a different form of light.

"Me either this day has taken me so long for us to get here but we're here and I'm glad this day has arrived." She said proudly then her mind went somewhere she didn't expected.

"What wrong? Your looking depressed." Her friend Brenda asked while checking her make up.

"Why you think that?" Asia said shaking off her feeling.

"Brenda, I see where you going with this so please don't go there in here of all days. Even I could see what's really on her mind but I don't want to pressure her about her feeling." I said rolling my eyes at her. I been around that queen Dashawn way too long, I don't even do this rolling eyes foolishness. More time will wash away the habits which he passed upon me.

"Okay, okay, okay this is my day so you two could save it til your not in the same room with me." Asia shouted with anger in her eyes carrying a pleasant tone in her voice.

I simply shook my head wearing a smile on my face cause I didn't even feel like talking about it on her beautiful day. Brenda had a shock expression on her face I knew good and well what was on her mind but she good people so I don't blame her reason for why she went there. Before she had the chance to respond there was a sudden knock on the door. I looked Brenda then at Asia when she said "Come in." When the door open a tall dark handsome brother stepped in.

"Hey, long time no see." He said nervesly.

"Why yes it has been. I'm glad you came it means a lot to me."

"Can we talk for just a moment Brenda and Boe?" He asked us and we just looked at her for her answer.

"No" Brenda and I replied in unison. I was wearing the hell out of this suit. Ain't no nigga was about to make me wear this fly gear for no wedding at all. Somebody was about to get married this day right here.

"Yo Boe, I ain't here to start no BS. All I wanna do is talk that's it."

For a almost thirty seconds there was dead silents among the three of us. "Just two minutes that's all your gonna get. You guys could you give us two minute." Asia said standing her ground placing her hands on her hips. Brenda and I give him an evil eye the whole time as we march of the room.

"You hear that ole boi?" I relied.

"Hear what?" I said looking a little puzzled at me.

"Tick, tick, tick... The timer counting down." I said then start grinning as I closed the door behind me and Brenda. I know it strange to start out your wedding day on a different note. This mess started out back in college but I don't think there any need for us to be going way back that far. After I moved from Savannah to Chicago, Illinois. The games we play. The people we used by hurting their emotions with our stupid ass act of pain. Back then is so laughable you wouldn't believe but now everything has turn into a complete mess.

Two years and a half earlier.

Monica Campbell stood behind Roc Blackwell while he unlocked his front door. As she waited her thoughts took her beyond the other side of the door thinking about his nine inch fat dick he had hanging between his legs which she saw throbbing though his jeans. "Hurry the fuck up." She demanded. They have been seeing each other for about two months she felt strongly for dark brother standing in front of her. This was the first time she had been invited to his apartment.

"I'm trying but this door wanna act up on a nigga." He said looking from the corner of his eye with a smirk on his face.

Finally the door open and she used both of her hands on his back then pushes him though the door smiling the whole time. Glancing around the room the first thing she noticed was a picture of some woman with him at a party. "Who is that chick in the picture baby?"

"What you talking about?" He said looking around the room till he saw what she was looking at then smiled. "Oh, that's my sister."

She sized him up and down not believing what he was saying at all cause they didn't resemble each other to say the least. She had only knew Roc for almost two months but she still couldn't tell if he was hiding something or not. Her eyes glued to his lips watching as he licked them making her moist between her legs. "Where were we just now?" She said forgetting what she was thinking he didn't respond he just lean over pressing his lips against hers.

"We were about to get undress." He said when there lips disconnect. Looking at her breast he could see the hardness of her nipple pressing though her blouse. "Starting with you."

"Who stopping you cause it's surely ain't me." She said walking pass him looking down the hall wondering how far the bedroom is. Then it hit her that she needed to use the bathroom. "I gotta freshen up real quick."

"Down the hallway to right, I'll meet you in the bedroom alright?" He utter watching as she walked down the hall then disappear into the bathroom. He then pulled out his cellphone looking though his contacts he find a name then started typing a text massage then press sent.

When Monica return to the room to find Roc seating on the edge of the bed waiting for her to come back in. Glancing around the room to find it neat which was odd for her cause most bachelors bedroom be in some kind of mess but not Roc Blackwell. Everything in place which made her wonder. She quickly brushed it off. "I'm hungry and I need for you to feed me now." She felt herself get moist again. Pulling her blouse over her head then letting her skirt dropped to the floor revealing her matching purple bra and pantie.

Roc rise off of the bed walked over to her then lifted her off of the ground into his arms then carry her over to the bed then placing her on it. Laying her on her back then he follow by kissing from her on the neck pausing on her beast. Hearing her moan in a low tone he continue to pleasure her by cupping her left beast with one and sucking on the other.

"Don't stop baby." She cried a little bite louder then before rocking her head from side to side grabbing the pillow. Never wanting his hands to stop touching her in all the right places. "Go lower baby, please I gotta feel that tongue inside of me."

Without saying anything he moved from her breast to between her cleavage kissing then licking at the same time causing her to moan louder. To him she tasted like strawberry only tab bite sweeter.

He didn't even say a thing about the fact that she has other dudes names on her legs even though she knew he seen them countless time. From men she been with though wrenched years but thought she was so completely love in with some so called Mr. Wright who she finds out in the end to be Mr. Wrong. Maybe this time it'll be different she thought to herself.

She felt him now between her legs and man this dude got her wide open in more ways than one. He buried his tongue deep inside her. "Yes, yes, yes... Please don't stop what your..." She said rolling her eyes to the back of her head.

"You like that don't you, Mo?" He asked looking up at her when she looked back up at him with pure lust in his eyes.

"You know I do but stop talking and do what you do best which is eating my pussy." She demand grabbing him by his head digging deeper into her lips below. She suddenly begin to come to a glazing all over her face squeezing the pillow as hard she could rocking her head side to side. Breathing hard speaking in tongue til finally blast a orgasm in his mouth.

About seventy minutes later Monica open her eyes to see Roc laying with his back to her, she reach and touched his back but he didn't respond must be sleeping she thought to herself. Rolling over she just to adjust herself in the bed next to him. Looking at the door of the bedroom thinking she heard a sound coming from down the hall but wasn't sure. She knew for sure the second time cause there were feet steps approaching the bedroom door. The door open to a female with a shock expression on on her face. There stood the same woman in the picture by the look in her eyes she ain't just a friend as he not too long ago told her. "What the fuck?" She yelled.

Roc jumped up off the bed putting on his boxers."Baby, it not what it looks like."

"Not what it looks like?" She repeated placing both of her hands on her hip as her eyes begin to water. "Looks like my husband fucking some little bitch in my bed. How could you do this to me. You promise to never hurt me."

Monica couldn't believe what her ears were telling her Roc is married. The few weeks they spent together nothing but a lies. She quickly got out of the bed feeling comfortable then begin put on her cloths which was near the door she frosted. "oh shit" she utter under hr breath.

"Bitch, you still here?" She said looking in her direction.

"I ain't no bitch I didn't even know he was marry." Monica said standing her ground. It wasn't even her fault she thought to herself.

She blast out laughing. "So you ain't told this *thing* your my husband, Steve?"

"Baby, she lying on me. You think I'll ever cheat on you when everybody knows me?"

"Yeah and why this slut is still in my bedroom?" She demanded reaching down and picking up her dress where she left it and throwing it at her. "Now get the fuck out my home before I do something crazy and bitch please don't test me."

Before she said anything snitch her dress up off the ground with her right hand then put it on her body as quickly as she could then grabbing her shoe off the floor walking past her down the hall storming like her life depended on it. Snitching her purse off of the table knocking over a picture to the floor slimming the door behind her. Listening as she stood at the elevator of his wife hitting and cruising him out. She even heard her calling him "son of a bitch" and "motherfucker." Even though she didn't like the bitch she was glad he was getting what he deserve it and then some.

Roc stood in the window looking for Monica outside as his woman stood a few feet away from him still yelling at him. He turn with a smirk on his face. "She gone."

She blast out laughing her head off. "Her dump ass really went for that?" She said when she manage to catch her breath leaning against a wall near her. "Boy, you know need to stop playing these games and be real with these females."

a few years ago   or so...

Roc and her have been friends ever since there college days when they shared a class together plus they kept on running into each other frat house parties all over campus.

"Hey short what your name" He said in her ear.

She turn her head around to face the voice in her her ear. To her surprise to see nice tall dark skin brother wearing a Roc a wear outfit. "Asia, and why you wanna that?"

"Cause I wanna know the name of the sexiest lady in the room. My name is..." He said but was cut off from finishing his sentence.

"I know who you are Roc." She said with a grin. "You been fucking one of my home girl and you in a few of my classes." Looking a little buzzed in the face.

"I am? I how have remember a woman as sexist as you are." He said in disbelieve lifting his right eyebrow. He was also empress by the fact that she knew who is was on campus. "Who is this friend of yours anyway?"

"Lakia Wiggins." Asia said proudly.

"We don't talk no more in fact it been a month." He said with a grin.

"Doesn't really matter cause you done fucked her. I don't date any man that deal with anyone of my friends. To be real I got a man on campus waiting on me." She said looking at one of her home girls weaving for her to come on. "Sorry but I gotta go, my ride is waiting on me. I'll see you around." She said then disappeared.

They did and somehow she turn into his first female friends. Even though they remind friends people all over campus thought there was something more going on.

"You think she'll call you like that chick Nai girl two years ago?" Asia said with a smirk which was truthfully colorful..

"Who knows but she got some dry pussy on her ass. I had to stay eating that dry ass pussy. Start to just fuck her in the shower."

"Like I wanna hear that shit." Asia said as she shook her head in not believing he just said that to her. "She could never be me." She paused for a brief second. "Cause I stay *wet.*"

"Hmm" He said. *Damn I wish she stop teasing a nigga* he thought to himself. What game is she really run on me.

"But you know I don't mess around with friends." Asia said with a grin lifting herself off the wall a few feet away from him. "What time you got Rocco?"

Glancing at his watch on his right waist then looked back at Asia. "It's a little after five. Why you asked?"

"Oh, snap I gotta go boy, have a date in a few hours." She said grabbing her purse off of the dresser as she headed out of the room down the hallway.

"Who is he this time?" He asked walking behind her.

She stop and then turn around to face him wearing a light smile. "Your daddy keep calling me so I'm gonna give him a chance after all. Hope he is worth the wait. Hmm...Think he can handle a chick like me?"

Roc couldn't do a thing but laugh for the simple fact that his father live over seas for the past two years. He and his father talk at least once or twice a month. "You got jokes now, I got you coming."

Asia open the front door still looking at him. "I have more don't test me."

"Bye Asia."

"Call me tomorrow."

"I'll do that." He said as he closed the door behind her he head in the direction of the bathroom once he was in he used his left hand to turn an the hot water adjusting it with his left hand once at a good temperature he took off his boxers then got in.

The later day...

Asia wore a dark blue DKNY outfit with black heels. Standing in front of the mirror putting on her black earring checking to make sure her make-up and hair just right. Yeah she was ready for another one of her dates with a complete loser. She knew it cause she was given his number from her home girl named Brenda who didn't have good taste in men. But hey she said the brother got money so you know she was down for a good meal plus it was free.

She arrived twenty minutes to soul food called *Angels Food*. It seem like a nice place to go since it's in midtown. How about this fool end up being thirty minutes late by then she done ate her mac & cheese and was in the middle of my oxtails over rice. Still sitting down at the table she give him a lite smile but it was crystal clear that she wasn't happy one bite. She already made up her mind that there wasn't gonna be a second date. "Must be John?"

He smiled still standing. "Yeah, yo ma sorry a nigga got off late." He said grabbing his chair from under the table. John was truly handsome as hell.

"You good I just started without you. Just because you can't be on time doesn't stop me one bit." Asia confessed honestly with a faded smile. She thought to herself they must not have a cellphone or your job don't have a phone obvious a lie."Are you from here?"

"Naw Brooklyn and yourself?"

"Yeah all my life except for when I lived in Atlanta four years when I was in college." She said then begin chewing on a piece of oxtail.

"I like your eyes." He said then licked lips.

"Thank you." She blushed. She could tell he was trying to go somewhere with this so lets see what's on his mind. Nothing good. "You don't look too bad yourself. So why you where late?"

"I had to work a little over, didn't want you thinking I was standing you up, so here I am.." He explained.

She lifted her right blow knowing it wasn't the truth cause of the simple fact he moved his face away a curtain as if he hiding from someone. These are the things that Rocwarned her about. The shit a nigga spit at a woman you wouldn't believe. She carefully watch him as his eyes wonder behind her then quickly come back to meet hers.

"Do you have any kids running around?" She asked playing her vibe she was reading from him was telling her she really didn't want to be there any longer.

"Two, a boy who is twelve and a girl who is three years old. I can tell you don't have any kids but do you like them." He said with a grin.

"Hell no." She said with an attitude wearing a brought a smile to her face. "I'm just joking I love children." She blast out laughing. *I could tell they aren't from the same woman I bet. He's a hoe for sure. I could tell from his fake ass swagger he has two or three bitches behind close doors. Hope he don't think he's getting me.* She thought to herself.

"I was about to say cause you don't look like the type of woman. How many do you want?" He said licking his lips then staring at her breast.

I hope he don't think he's getting any from me if so he got me fuck up. He must've been on that shit like a motherfucker. Ha ha ha Ashton where you at cause I know this a prank. She thought. "Two maybe three." Asia said but was thinking to herself that not with you. "Same momma?" Knowing the answer in her head.

Before he could answer a plus size woman walked up to the table with arms fold wearing a mean mug on her face. He jumped up out of his seat before she could speak. "Baby, it's not what it look like."

"What the fuck your ass doing here? You said you were going to the store for some cigarette." The woman yelled at him forgetting that she were in a restaurant where people begin looking in their direction.

Asia begin to look in her purse till she found a twenty dollar bill. She got out her seat then walked away to the cashier handing her waitress explaining what she paying for then she was out of there. It's funny how life works out here she was playing games earlier now look what happen to her. "I'm gonna get you Brenda just wait till I see you." She uttered under her breathe as she walked down the she.

Brandon sat on a bench in the park near the playground waiting for Asia. They met here for their walk around the park which they did once a month ever since he moved up there three months ago. Sniffing a lily which was plated about two feet away. An elderly man was walking his dog past came past him. That dog barked at every person that cross it's path, it seem like the only thing the damn the thing did other than stare. *You little bitch you better get the fuck on with your business cause I ain't the one to be reckon with so get the hell out of my face.* He thought to himself as the people went on along there way. Children running playing among each other.

Feeling his cellphone ringed in his back pocket brought me back to reality. Pulling out he saw it says it was Khalid. Wearing a huge smile on his face. "Hey baby, everything okay?"

"I was just calling to check on you." He says in his deep soothing voice.

"I'm fine sitting here thinking about you and life. It's too beautiful out here. I'm so glad you and I decided move here. Not gone front to you about this but I do miss April and a very small part I mean a very very small part of the good old me misses Dashawn. That's real fucked of me to even consider missing that motherfucker after he tried his best to take me off the face of this earth." He said with a smile fading from my lips hate admitting stupid shit like that came out of his mouth. So many times he thought about everything that went down in Savannah and how it went up in flames like his home. He always had a back up plan when it came to chaos. Jermaine came to his mind he quickly shook him out of his thoughts by changing the subject to something that was in enlightening. "What you doing anyway?"

"What the fuck I told you about mentioning those two faced piece of shit so drop it. I'm just straightening up the front room. How bout we have launch downtown later?" He asked sounding like something was on his mind.

"Sounds like you got a plan and I'm game just let me know the time and place." He said shifting himself on the bench away from the sun in his eyes.

"Eleven and the waffle house downtown ."

"Baby, just enough time to do what I gotta do. See you then bye." He said then end the call.

Khalid and Brandon have been together for six years in about in bout a month. He has truly been a blessing to him. Whenever he needed him he'd be there without him asking him. He got my own money and he got his own but if he didn't know Brandon got his as well. He'll fight for him if anybody dares fuck with him.

Finally Asia appeared down the side walk from a distinct. They get together to talk about everything since they don't talk that much doing the month. Getting up out of the place where he was sitting on the bench with the brightest smile on his face. "Hey you. I thought you forgot about me for a second there."

"You know I can't do that to my good old friend." Asia chuckle leaning in to give Brandon a hug. "Nice outfit."

"Thanks." He was wearing red sweat suit with matching red and white New Balance. She was wearing tight black sweat pants and a white tank top with hair in a neat ponytail. "You don't look too bad yourself. So what dash?"

"Work is getting back on track. I have two new clients coming in later this week which is a good on the hand my dating life needs a little work." She explains about her jacked up date last night.

"No shit." He blast out laughing my head off. "I just know you ain't go out like that, tell me it isn't so?"

"Yeah Boe, he tried the shit out of me. Thank god I got a straight man to school me bout niggas like him." She said with a smirk on her face as they walk down the sidewalk. Looking at me as I looked   in another direction. "What?"

"Nothing" Was the only word that came out his mouth for belief second. "Your starting to glow again over *Roc* . Why don't you just fuck each other and get it all over with. I mean he's the same way about you. Better get off your high horse and get the dick and stop playing. You two would make a cute couple but I get it why you don't wanna go with him. The man is a bite of a slut."

"Boe, I told you time and time again that I don't mess around with friends man. And I plan on keeping it that way."

"Asia, you and old girl ain't even friends anymore so what you excuse now. In fact you two hadn't even spoken since her got ex spelled a year later. "

"It doesn't matter if we ain't friends anymore so just drop it. Alright!!!" Asia said with a attitude rolling her eyes.

"Damn, you really getting bothered about your feeling for Rocl see.." He said grinning from ear to ear.

"You know what go find somebody to play with." She murmured. Claiming her nerves just a bite. "So what going on with you?"

He suddenly got quit looking at a cute couple from walking past them. "Well, everything with me and Khalid okay."

"Is okay?" She question him.

"Yeah it okay, I mean what you do you want me to say?" He replied.

Asia didn't say a word but she did give him a look that said it all. Her mind drifted a far away place. "Nothing. It just you weren't so secretive about your relationship before."She said finally shaking her head in disbelief.

"Our relationship been kind a weird we been a secret for so long it's hard to be real about our feeling toward each other. I'm trying and he trying it just crazy like that." He said with a blank stare on his face. He promised myself that he'll never tell anyone his business ever since dealing with Dashawn and April. The way they both betrayed my trust and faith in them.

"Everything gonna work it's self out just trust in him cause it looks like he has true feeling for you."

"I know he does." He said blushing.

"So what your really worry about?" She asked digging into deeper repress side of me which I kept bury within.

Asia isn't a thing like April she is more of a listener. She encourages me to be stronger which was one of the reason why he decided to moved from Savannah. They decided together that it would be better start over in a new place. Asia never knew he will never know our secret life. It took us a few years to build this and he ain't plan on fucking that up. For real. He is ready for whatever came their way.

"Are you listening to the words that are coming out my mouth?" She asked awaking me from a deep trance.

"What was the question?" He asked but realized before she'd even mention a thing. "Oh, maybe it's nothing at all."

"What the hell?" Asia said coming to a completely stop with a shock expression.

When he turn around to see the object she had her eyes on then he even got speechless it was none other than Manuel Parker. Manuel was her college and high school sweet heart who she broke up while she was in her last year of college to pursue his career in football. He got a injury about a year ago then moved back to start his life over.

"We could just turn around if you wanna." Brandon subjected giving gentle touch on her right shoulder wearing a concern in my voice.

"I think that would be best." Was the only thing came out of her mouth. The rest of the walk was pretty much died after that. When we were done we made plans later on this week that were gonna have lunch before parting our ways.

Not even paying any attention to the woman who obviously eying him like he was a piece of meat. Their are all the same he thought to himself wanting his money. He was really wanting to settling down not in the mood for a topical woman want nothing but his money. He knew that he done lost the real thing when he dumped her back in college.

Asia Gray was the one he let get away and every piece of him called out to her since the day he left to start his career in NFL. Seeing the tears rolling down her face that dreadful day. What can I say I wasn't ready to give my life in the light he thought to himself. The lime light wasn't what he thought it was gonna be but in the end it was anything but what he thought it would be.

From a far he could see a female who reminded him of Asia. Then all those memory came rushing back to him like it just happen yesterday. He wondered if she ever find out he was back would she ever forgive him for the wrong he done to her? Maybe not but he'll never know if don't find her.

A group of women came running over to see if they could get a autograph of him and maybe a picture. Not wanting to be bothered he begin jogging in the another direction just to avoid them. Beside dealing with them he got some business to handle later on he had a meeting with some business adviser down town.

Asia arrived home about thirty five minutes later. Before she had a chance to take off her tank top she was stopped by a ranging phone in the living room. "Hello?"

"How was last night?" A female voice says though the phone.

"I'm gonna beat your fucking ass." She blurted out. "Next time you make sure nigga know how to be on time."

"I told him you like for a man to be late. So how long did you waited for him?" Brenda asked with a grinning.

"That shit ain't funny Brenda. Plus he has the nerve to be looking around the room at other bitches."

"He didn't seem like the type to do a sister like that." Brenda says in dis believe.

"And you ready for the *hell no*?" She asked getting ready to blow her nerve.

"It couldn't get any worse then that Asia."

"Yeah it did."

"What happen next?" Brenda said disappointed.

"A big woman show whopping and shouting at his ass. I'm like you got a bitch." She said as she sat in a nearby chair.

"Hold up, what you trying say about a BIG WOMAN. We can handle nigga very well thank you." She said with a slight attitude at Asia.

"I wasn't trying to offend you so you can bring that down a notch please."

"Whatever, I'm just saying but that bitch ass nigga got what coming to him. He and I will cross path very soon. I'll make it my job to do so."

"Back to the drawing board for me."Asia said looking at watch lifting herself off of the sofa deciding to end the conversation. "I'll check at you later gotta go show a house to some clients out on the south side."

"You better call me, bye." Brenda said then they disconnect the call on both end.

Asia undressed then got herself in a shower. While she wash her body her thoughts took her over of thoughts Manuel. He still looked good and even improved in some areas. Before she knew it she was playing with herself uncontrollably. Noticing what she was doing she'd automatically stop wash him out of her mind.

About two weeks later...

Roc Blackwell and cousin Zeus Eastwood standing in the line inside of Footlocker. He wanted the hot new pair of *Air Jordan* that came about three hours ago. After standing in a long line for so long it was worth it in the end cause they are too fly he thought to himself. He was telling Zeus bout his weekend.

"So has she called since you have her running half naked?" Zeus chuckle.

"Naw, she hasn't call like those crazy chick in the past." Roc said with a odd look on his face thinking about the few women in the past. One bust out his window, flatten his tires, and even showed up to one of his classes he was teaching good thing she waited outside till class was done.

"I wish I had a *friend* like Asia." Zeus said between chuckles. "You and her need to stop beating around bush and just hook up for gods sakes. Yo, why you ain't hit that yet?"

"Zeus, I don't think it'll happen in this lifetime for the simple fact that were just friends and friends don't fuck. So she say every time." He told him along with his ego.

"Tell me anything but that doesn't mean I'll believe you. I mean she ain't putting out cousin or your game isn't that good?" Zeus asked.

"She wanna be friends and she don't sleep with her friends ex." He explained.

"You slept with one of her home girl?" Zeus asked wide eying him. "Man you a hoe."

"Man, I done told you the story and ain't plain on telling yo ass no more." Roc said with a attitude. "So hows the wife?" He said changing the subject cause he was tired of having a conversation about Asia.

"She good. We not talking about my Lily were talking about girl your Asia and you." He said knowing what Roc was doing.

They walked out leaving the Footlocker head back to Roc 2009 Expedition when two honeys came approaching there way. Roc noticed one them giving him a district look then looked away saying something to her friend grinning as they pasted them by. "What's up shortie? What your name is?"

One of them turn around pointing a finger at herself. She could tell by the way he shook his finger signaling for her. She knew he was talking about her friend. "Girl, he talking bout you not me."

"Candy, why you wanna know?" She question him removing some hair out of her face so she can see him clearly.

"Cause I wanna know that's why. You must not be from around here."

"What makes you think that?" She asked rolling her eying at him then sucking her teeth.

"Cause you don't look like it that's why." He teased.

"Well damn you got a lot nerve to think that, must not have good vocabulary I see." She said laughing glancing his cousin then at her home girl. "Girl, he didn't even tell me his name ain't that some shit."

"I'm a professor so you know I could go there with words. You asked mine but I'll give it to you anyway, my name is Roc."

"Roc, common name for a uncommon boy." She teased at him in a way that turned him on without a doubt. Rolling her eyes as she placing one of her hands on her hip. "Sweetie bounce."

"Well, I can't get a number or something?" He said.

"Huh, no I don't think so sweetie."

"Why not?" Roc asked her looking her dead in the eye.

"You must really think your all that cause your sporting a fly ass outfit that type of shit don't mean a thing to me. I'll catch you on the flip side." Candy said cutting her eyes at him then leaving him standing there wearing a stupid expression on his face.

"Can you believe these chicks these days cuz?" Roc said in disbelieve of what just happen. No women ever dis him like that before.

"Believe it cause it just happen to you." Zeus said between chuckles at him. After seeing the look on Rocface he straighten his face as best as he could. Deep down his pride bruised. Zeus tried his best cheer him up. "Man, don't be sweating chick cause you know she just playing hard to get that's all."

"But it was something about her man, you just don't get it." He protected. As the made there way to his 2009 Expedition. They got in but still Candy was on his mind. He never been dis by any female before except for once back in high school and Asia in college. It bothered him deeply he know deep in his mind that he had to get this Candy. His cell ringed breaking his train of thought when he saw Asia name on the caller I.D his whole attitude changed and Zeus spotted it from the corner his eye. "What sup Asia?"

"Nothing much just called to check up on you. So what going on with ya?" Asia says into the phone as *Da Brat* old jams *Funkdafied* blaze through the phone he couldn't help but hear it.

"Ain't nothing just chilling with Zeus. I just came from getting my new kicks which I'm gonna be rocking tonight at the club. Wanna come with us?" He said knowing her answer before she even speak.

"Yes, I would love to but I made plans with Brenda." She said thinking about the club days she haven't been to one in about a two years or so. The scene gotten old after she left college and join the real world.

"Well bring Brenda with her fine."

"You know she can't bring her little girl to the club." Asia said adding an eight year old girl the conversation. "I'll see if she'll get a babysitter at the last minute if that makes you any feel any better."

"Yeah we'll see." He said with a slight attitude and it show in his eyes. "Asia, I holla at you later alright?"

"Talk with you later, bye." She said then disconnect there conversation. She look over her shoulder at Brenda who was changing the cd to old school music from the eighty. "I can't believe that you still listen to that girl."

"Bitch, don't hate on my music your ass could learn some shit from *Betty Wright.*" Brenda sucked her teeth then press play on the entertainment system then begin rocking to *Clean up Woman* with her back to Asia.

"Whatever you ready yet?"

"Give me a few minute,why?" Brenda said looking back at her.

"Nothing you know I don't like being for the movie."

"It's more than that just spill the beans and stop beating around the bush." Brenda stop dancing folding her arms with a serious expression which meant she business.

"Okay, it was Rocas always tripping for the simple fact that *I* don't want to go a clubs. I'm not about that scene anymore I got bills to pay." She confessed.

"Girl, he properly want you to let your hair down that's all. Shit I wanna go to one myself need a man to buy me a drink and pay a bill or two." Brenda begin laughing when she saw that Asia begin grinning.

"You is too much for me to even try an handle." Asia mention that Rochad invited her to join them. "We're gonna be late for the movie if you don't hurry up."

Brenda grabbed her purse and keys off of the table next to the flat screen TV then looked in the mirror to see if hair was in place. She wear a red blouse top with back apple black bottom jeans heels to match both colors. "Sexy is ready to go so get your ass up."

He was the kitchen frying chicken listening to Jazz. He was wearing one of Khalid favorite outfit which was nothing but a blue apron that says 'hot chef cooking' with nothing but a thong on underneath with my pulled back in a ponytail. He was expecting him to show up any minute now. He walked out just for second to set the table lighting two candles then returning to just in time to take the meat out of the grease. He felt a present creep up behind him grabbing him around his waist kissing him on his neck. "You late." Was the only thing that reach his lips with Khalid arms still wrapped around him. So tight he could feel his erection on his plump ass through his gym shorts which turn him on.

"Our game ran late my bad." Khalid said getting a firm grip of my ass. "Did you miss me baby?"

He placed a lid on top of the frying pan after turning off the stove he finally turn his body around to face Khalid. "You know I did cause I go crazy when your gone more then an hour." Glazing deep into his eyes. "I got the pot of Cajun rice, green beans and the cornbread is in the oven. Khalid please take a shower cause you starting smell." He said tooting his nose cause of the smell from him.

"I'm bout to but I'll be leaving in an hour and a half for a business trip." He said turning his back walking towards the bathroom with me on my tail.

"Where to?" He asked. "You didn't mention anything about going any place."

"Savannah. Something I gotta check up on and it just came up."

"You normally tells me in advice before you up and leave. Why all of a sudden you got business to handle. I hope your not going down there..." He paused when he reach to doorway.

"Stop tripping ain't nobody going there for that so just chill the fuck out." He said with a attitude then begin taking off his clothes dropping them on the floor layer by layer.

"What's going with us don't you love me anymore?" He said with concern in his eyes wondering what he was thinking. Since leaving Savannah their relationship has taken a strange turn that he didn't expected at all. For seven years he never acted discreet, but loving, caring, and everything that a man could even come close to. The love, hate, hot, and cold act is truly begin to drive him delirious.

"Ain't nothing going on with us just us so just stop tripping it cause you bugging." He said turning the water on then getting in the shower ending there conversation. After he wash and dry then dressed he return to the dining room where Brandon was sitting just waiting for him it wasn't til he blessed the food before ate. In the middle of their meal he finally broken the silent between them. "Is you gonna be like this till I leave?"

"It depends when are you gonna act like my man instead of a stranger in our house. I love you so much that I'll do just about anything for you and you know that. We been closed ever since our first day here. I still think about those good times we shared before then."

"Those times has come and gone. So stop tripping like your doing right now."

"Oh I'm tripping." Noticing that he didn't even bother to say *I love you to, baby.* Maybe he is bugging about the whole thing or maybe it's him that is not paying attention to the distance us both are making by not trying their best to do what they do. "You know what let talk about something else like when you be coming back home."

He thought for a second as if searching for the right words to say. "About two days or less. I'm trying to return as fast as I can."

A smile touched Brandon lips as a scent of comfort came over him. "I am truly gonna miss you while your gone you just don't know don't know how much. Hurry back my Ruff Rider."

"I know." He says in a cocky tone wearing slight smile. "I'll miss you too." He admitted bluntly without a second thought.

"The photographer will be here next Friday at two o'clock." He said not looking in his direction but down at his food as he ate.

"Yeah whatever." He said nonchalance.

"I mean if you don't wanna do this just tell me. The only reason I wanted this to be done is because there no picture of us that says we are a couple."

"You know I gotta go my plane leave in forty-five minutes so I needs to head out. Your gonna drive me to the airport right?" He says ignore his question by changing the subject. They made small talk about the house work that need to be done and they both agreed to work on them as a couple. They pulled up in front of the airport. "I'll call you when the plane lands. Alright?"

Brandon picked up his cell and dial up number then wait for the caller to answer the phone. "What you doing?"

"I'm just leaving the movie theater with Brenda. Why? We bout to go to a bar where Rocand Zeus was be partying at for the night. " Asia responded.

"You going a *club*?" Brandon says in a shocking tone not believing that his friend was going to a club of all places. "I wanna come."

"Where you man at?" She asked.

"He had a last minute business call to make that got him on a plane heading out. How fast can you meet me at my town house?"

"In a little over twenty minutes or so."

"I'll meet you there before you get there. I'll see you then alright." He said then they said there byes then disconnected there conversation. About thirty minutes later he open the front door to see Asia and a female a long side her. "Come in please." Stepping aside to let them cross the threshold.

"Boe, this is Brenda Valentino and Brenda this is my is my college buddy Brandon but he goes by Boe." Asia said introducing them to each other.

"Nice to me I heard so much about you. She didn't say it right called me Boe if your ghetto." He said bring a smile to his face.

"Same here I was begin to think that you were a ghost. All I hear is Boe this and Boe that." She started laughing when she saw Asia and Brandon laughing.

"I must be really be the it for me to be chatting about you a lot." Asia said looking at Brandon. She didn't realize how much she talked about him but he was a cool lay back kinda guy with his head on his shoulders. If you had any type of problems a question bout a man Brandon was your guy.

Roc has been at the club for about an hour and already received five numbers. Zeus on his cell every ten minutes with his wife of five years. Roc always saw himself as the no marrying kind for the sample fact that he didn't want to settle down. He give him a quick look shaking head in disapproval. Every time the song change he'd find a chick with a phat booty he come up taking her by the arm then grind on half the the time dance. It wasn't till about twelve-thirty or so when glanced at the entrance spotted Asia, Brenda, and Brandon walking as one unit. "It must be gonna rain this morning cause you never come out."

"Well Brenda had wanted to come then Boe called cause he wanted to have some fun so you know we had to scoop him up." She explain with a smile.

"It took Brenda, Boe, and myself just so you could bring your ass out to the club. Look like you need a drink. Let me go get you a drink stay here." He said then disappear into the crowed retrieve her beverage.

Brandon looked at Brenda tooting up his lips making a face. "Now Brenda, you know that was mess up?"

"Sure was but he always doing that shit like that it doesn't even bother me anymore." Brenda looking back at him.

"What are you two talking about?"

"We ain't been here in a hot second and you get a nigga to buy you a drink. Not any one but Roc. He see two other people standing right beside you. He could've brought Brenda one as well." Brandon said with a grin.

"Okay." Brenda chime in.

From distance Brandon saw Roc approaching them. "Know what Brenda, let me take you over there so that I could buy you a drink." Looping his arm with hers then left her leaving standing there alone till Roc accompany her.

"Where did they go off to?" Roc asked handing her her drink which was was a double vodka and cranberry.

"They hating cause got me a drink and didn't offer to buy them a thing." Asia grinning. She and Roc carry there conversation over to a empty booth.

Brenda went on the dance floor with some dude that brought her a drink at the bar. Zeus was chatting with Brandon when he wasn't texting his wife. Asia called having a drink in her hand every twenty minutes then hitting the dance floor with just about any guy that would asked her. Leaving the club Brenda ride with Zeus cause they stay on the same side of town. Brandon drive himself home and Asia ride with Roc in her Camry she decided stayed spend the night at his place.

"Thanks for letting me stay here again. Good looking out for your girl." She said reaching for a glass of water in his kitchen.

"What are friends for?" He says in a seductive tone sitting in the sofa.

"A very *attractive* friend that is too fucking *fine* for his own good." She said taking a few steps closer to him. Not thinking but speaking in fact she said the first thing that came to her mind.

"Well tell me how you really feel about me." He joked but wanted to know what she thoughts of him deep down. His mother use to always tell him *a drunk person tells no lies*.

"I wonder is you a good kisser and what could you do with your big fat ass tongue." She said batting her eyes at him rubbing on his right thigh. To her surprise he leaned over giving him a passionate kiss she didn't expect him to act on. She tried to pull him off but begin to enjoy his lips on hers the next thing she knew she had started undressing him.

"Do you really wanna open Pandora's box cause there is no going back?"

"Stop talking you might just miss your chance be inside me. You and I both know that we need this." She said leaning in again for another kiss forgetting her rules for only one night. When she awoke early the next morning realizing what she'd done when Roc naked body laying near hers. She eased out of the bed. Putting on her clothes as fast as she could making sure she didn't woke him. It wasn't till noon when Roc called when she saw it was him she'd avoided his call.

For the next two days Asia did everything in her power to avoid Roc but he made that hard to do, calling her non stop around the clock. Every hour he would sent her emails messages saying "call me." She refused without a second thought. Even when she went to bed he was there in her dreams kissing her in all the right places which was making her moist in all the right places.

She decided on the third day to have lunch with Brandon and Brenda just to get her mind off him but it still didn't work. Brenda was laughing to a joke that Brandon had said. Everyone was laughing but Asia.

"Are you okay?" Brenda asked wondering what was going though her mind and why was she acting so differently.

"I'm fine, why you ask me that?" Asia asked snapping back into the conversation looking back at her.

"Look like something on your mind." She snapped back.

"Nothing wrong with me."

"Huh, if you wanna play that game it's on you but don't expect me to protect or help you if don't to talk about it." Brandon said with a mean mug on his face sensing that underneath the surface she wasn't giving up so easily. He was good on reading people.

"I don't wanna talk about it cause it's to disturbing to even try and talk about." She said rolling her eyes hard.

"Try me." They said in unison with face starring back at her wearing a straight face.

"I bet I'll figure it out before Brenda." Brandon said with smirk on his face looking back Brenda who had blank expression on her face.

"Why you tryina put a bet on her life?"

Waiter came up giving them there breakfast. Brenda scrambles eggs with cheese grits, then Asia has the waffles and some strawberry on the side, and last but least Brandon had scrambles eggs mixed with some shrimps, sausage, and bacon with gravy poured it.

"As I saying," Brandon thought for a second then said with a smile. "I'm good with reading people watch and learn. I'm good at what I do."

"Wanna put your money where your mouth is?"

"Don't write no check that your ass can't cash. Cause you will be broke fucking with me."

"Oh, you two tryina use my situation for some money?" Asia said with shock in her eyes wearing a light grin not believing what she was hearing.

"I stay using my physiology skills." Brandon grinned uncontrollably ignoring her statement.

"Well," She begin wondering where she was going to begin telling her story without them finding out what she done. "Have you ever done something that you couldn't take back. I just wish that I never forgot my rule this one night I swear I'll never do it again." She said the tears begin to fall from her eyes.

"Is this over that Manuel cause I know you said that you saw him the other day." Brenda said thinking that she won the bet with a priceless.

"No."

"Of coarse it's not him. Girl, you ain't even listen to how she speaking and acting. She getting tense her body is. So I know for sure that your tensing over a man without a doubt in my mind." Brandon said glancing at Brenda then at Asia.

"Okay it's a man alright but you don't know who it is I'm referring to."

"Now, the next thing is you said rule and how you don't like breaking them. And you haven't broken any of them before until." Brandon paused watching her expression then proceed. "There only one rule which is the powerful one of them all which is sex."

"You still didn't say a name smarty pants." She said she just knew he wouldn't figure out what she was.

"Roc." He said opening his hand for twenty from Brenda.

"Damn you good better than I thought. So when did this happen Asia?" Brenda said reaching in purse for the twenty dollars handling it over to him.

"Girl, they been friends for years since college back in the days. He use to date Lakia chick that she use to be friends with. Asia, made a rule that she'll never mess around with a friend of hers man which I don't understand since they stop being friends all those years ago. I knew it would've happen sooner or later. It just took a drunk night at the club then leaving spending the night at Roc place. Silly girl, you can't fool me for one minute." Brandon said placing the money back in his wallet then went back to finish off his breakfast.

"So what you gonna do about it." Brenda murmured to Asia.

"That's the million dollar question."

"Call him and see what's up with him."Brenda suggested.

"Brenda, she didn't call nor answered his phone call. Avoiding the issue the way you should handle this situation. I mean handle it like a strong independent woman I know for all these years. You never know what may come out of the this."

"And how can't you be so sure about this?"

"Asia, I could see since college this dude had feeling for you. You were just always blocking him out of your system but still wanted him. Just be real about how you feel."

"What he said. I got one question and you know what that is don't you?" Brenda said wanting to know the details.

"That dick was too good I mean I see why these hoes be going crazy over him." Asia said then all of them bust out laughing.

"Your body says it was more then that so stop fronting and spill the beans." Brandon said with a priceless smile on his face. Knowing once again everything was getting juicy which made him happy cause just about everything was moving slow to him in this town. She told them all this glorious details about Rocdown to how big it was as how well he did it.

"It was better than I have ever imagine and then some."

"So tell me this would you do it again?" Brenda said lifting an brow.

"That is a good question." Brandon chime in.

"I don't know what to tell you the truth about it." She confessed. She never intended to go that far in the first place she just wasn't thinking clearly at all and needed to clear her thoughts.

Brandon eyed his watch wondering why haven't heard from Khalid. It's been three days he haven't even called yet. Deciding to reach into his pocket pulling out his cell he called him not wanting to wait another minute longer. "What up?" He says into his ear sounding displeased by him even calling him at all.

"Did I catch you at a bad time babe?" Brandon said softly into the phone with his eyes back on Brenda and Asia.

"You good. What you doing?"

"Chillin with some friends. I wanted you to meet them their really cool people. I want us to have to have a dinner real soon with some of mine with some of yours." He said exhaling looking in another direction.

It was so silent that he could hear a door closed in the back round. "Whatever you want baby. I'll be home in a little bite."

"Okay, I'll see you when I get there." He said before say their goodbyes then he disconnected there conversation. Bringing his mind back to their attention by placing a fake smile on his face. "So what I missed?"

"Nothing much but Brenda little angel being in a play." Asia said with a smile thinking about Brenda little girl and how she would wanna have a child one day.

"She suppose to play the fairy godmother." Brenda added in. "It's gone be in next month so your ass better there nigga."

"Let me know in I'll be there with my flowers for her." He said glancing at his watch once more then back at him. "But I better get going cause I gotta met my man before he gets there."

"We need to do this again very soon." Brenda suggested.

"Not a bad idea." Asia said.

"I'm game just let me know when, Asia you got my number give it to Brenda." Brandon said as he picked up his belonging saying his good bye then disappearing though the double doors.

Brandon was sitting in front of his computer when Khalid creep up behind him. He still didn't know that he even came in till Khalid placed a kiss on his cheek. Caught off guard by him he'd quickly change the computer scene to something else. "You really scared me coming in like you did but then again that's so like you."

"You know how I do it. I guess your working on your top secret book, huh?" He said with a light smile glancing at the screen.

"You know I'm not ready for ya to see any of it just yet so back away from my laptop. I'll be off in just two minutes if you can wait." He said blocking him away from the screen playfully.

"Only for you I can wait in the bedroom." He said walking toward the direction of the bedroom once in the doorway he paused. "In the bed." Speaking in a seductive tone then begin walking away once more. "Didn't I mention I will have no clothes on."

"Hard I hope." Brandon said in a low tone that was heard by Khalid but he didn't respond. *I hope he didn't see what I was doing. Naw if he did he would've said something about it, you know he not that quiet about his emotion. He been the same man for the past few years. He loves himself some me he'll do anything for me why cause he loves how you mind fuck him.* He thought to himself.   Finishing his work on his laptop closing it when done with the work. Taking off his clothes before leaving the room as he made his way down the hallway the only thing that was on his mind healing, sexual healing in every way possible. Pushing anything that would change is mind somewhere else out before it even had a chance to enter his thoughts. Standing in the doorway wearing a priceless smile looking at Khalid looking back a him like he were

a little boy getting his favorite toy.

Asia stood with intention all over her body from head to toe out Roc . She

called him letting him know she was going to drop by around eight o'clock pm. After the

first knock on the door he open and greeted her without a second thought. After

standing in the doorway for only a minute she cleared her throat. "Well aren't you gone

invite me in?"

"My bad." Was the only thing he said as he moved a step back so she could

get in. "So can I get you a beer or something."

"No. I think there is something we need to talk about." She said looking in

another direction then back at him sadly. *I hope this goes well cause I don't wanna loose*

his friendship over a drunken night of sex which I was too intoxicated to think straight.

Here goes nothing. She thought to herself exhaling hard. "You see I don't think that it

would be a good thing for us to do what we did the other night again. I just think we

should be friends and nothing else."

"I was thinking the same thing I had too much to drink you... I mean we went

too far and I knew if we weren't thinking clearly." He said lying to himself. True is he

always saw himself with her ever since their college days. After trying for so long he did

what most men do in that situation he give up.

"So..." She said with a paused looking in another direction. "how everything

going for you? I know I haven't been calling and checking in like I usually do."

"Everything is everything with me. What about you?" He murmured to her which she barely hear.

"Business is going kind of slow at the moment but I supposed to be hosting a open house. So you better tell all your other professional buddies to bring there wallets." She said with a fake smile folding her to chest tightly.

"Tell me what time and the place my guys will be there." He said with a weird expression that she couldn't read. "I suppose to meet the boys at the bar down the street." He said turn his body toward the front door and he didn't look back at her til he open the door.

She walked in the hallway turning back around to face him one last time before she left wearing a light smile. "Call me tomorrow so we could meet up for lunch or something."

He gave her a nod then close the door with her still looking at him. She knew he didn't like what she said to him to be truthful to herself she didn't either but being friends with him all these years she saw how he played games with other women. Even though she join in his games plenty of times though the years she never did a guy like that but then again she hadn't never been in a relationship that lasted long since the break up a few years ago.

When she'd arrived home about twenty later to find the phone ringing like crazy. Rushing to answer but the answering machine came on which made her slow down.

"HEY THIS ASIA Gray AT THE BEEP LEAVE ONE."

"What up shortie? I know you didn't expect to be hearing my voice after all this time..." Her heart skip a beat causing her to drop her purse and cellphone the floor. He was right for thinking that she didn't expect to hear Manuel Parker voice ever again. "well I wanna see you. You know...catch up for old time sack. I know you current boyfriend don't get mad if he hear this message but I had to see how you were doing these. When you get this give me a call at..." He said leaving a message to contact him then disconnected.

She plopped herself in the nearest chair in the room. She just couldn't believe the voice which she heard that is still echoing in her ear. *I just can't believe that motherfucker just called me. He got some fucking balls to dial my number. Fuck that bitch ass nigga. Got to be eating shit or smoking weed or something. Shit something got him to build up the nerve to call me.* She thought to herself. She got up and left the living room walking to the kitchen opening up one of the cabinet to fix herself a drink which she hadn't done since the night she went out. "I gotta get this Manuel Parker off my mind. " She said aloud shaking her head in disbelieve of how her night went.

About three weeks later...

Brandon repeatedly eyed his watch then stared at the fronted door like clock work while photographer continue to set up his gear. So he finally open up his cell to call him for the third time in an hour. But he didn't bother to answer his cell or return his call. *You know what the show gonna start without Khalid presents. He on some other shit and I don't have time to be following him up. How long must do I got I got to deal with his twisted ways.* Looking in the direction of the photographer who appears to be done setting up. Wearing a devilish smile changing bringing his eyes back to life. "Sorry, my man ain't coming so you got me all to yourself."

Raul was his name he stood at about the same height as him red boned with his broad shoulder hazel eyes. "It all good with me you already paid so let me know when your ready." He says in his deep and sexy tone winking his right eyes at him.

Feeling a slight breeze go up his spine blinking seductively at Raul. "I been born ready for the camera I'm just waiting for you. So start." He demanded as he processed to give him a look.

Raul took shot after shot in different poses. To him Brandon was a natural in front of the camera cause of his personalty. He sight at him thinking to himself.

"What's wrong?" He said with a curious expression on his face taking his left hand scratching his head then fold his arms tightly to his chest.

"hmm, something missing." He said searching with his around the room when he found a spot. "Go over to the window I wanna run with a ideal. If ya game?"

Without a word he walked over to the window. "I'm always game so what else you want me to do?" *Please tell me to take off something. Khalid would really love that kind of shit then he'll think twice about standing me up knowing that I don't like that bullshit. If this photographer wasn't so fine I'd be really mad right at him.*

"Lay just like that a pond the glass then look like thinking about something serious." He said as he begin once more to take picture of him. "Now put your hand on the glass."

The feeling of being board came over him it was then that he felt lonely. From a distinct he could hear the front door open and then close knowing that means that Khalid was there. A completed smile come to his lips before he even step foot in the living room. "My bad, my meeting run later then I expected it to but I'm here now."

"Sweetie, you good come over here before he run out film." Brandon said as he made his way over to him placing a kiss on his cheek wrapping his arms around his waist. "I'm glad your here."

About thirty minutes or so later Raul was finished and packed up his equipment. "I'll call you on Monday so you could decide what the next move."

"Will do." Khalid says in a cocky tone.

"Glade you made up here without any trouble Raul. I hope all of them came out just fine. Baby, I got a feeling the picture I've taken will blow your mind." Brandon said placing his arm around his waist resting his head on the shoulder. *Did I miss something here could Khalid be on the jealous side over Raul but there was nothing to be jealous about.*

After Raul left there was silence in the room and they didn't know where to start. Walked off to the bedroom then begin undressing himself he thought that Khalid would follow but he had other plans instead in fact when he return to the living room to find a note saying that he was head out for a while.

Bachelors with deep pocket wondered around checking out the four bedroom two and a half bathroom huge living and dinning with a view of the city. They was ladies there as well but not as much of the men. Asia was thrilled to see the outcome of her event wearing a confident smile, it has only been an hour and she has six potential buyer two of them was friends of Rocwho she has talk to much pryer to the open house. Brandon and Brenda showed up to give there friend support which she needed without a doubt.

Asia exit out of the bathroom to find a stranger waiting for her with his in his pocket wearing Joseph Abboud suit. She confronted him she could not to let him know that she was bothered by the present of the stranger without a question in her mind. "Manual, what a surprise to see you how you find me?"

Manual smile putting all his white teeth on display something he put pride in taking care of. "I heard from old friend that it'll be a open house but honestly didn't know you were going to be here."

"I know you don't think I'm falling for that mess you spit my way, cause I know you had to know that I was hosting this open house." She murmured to him.

"Okay, I tried to call you but you didn't responded."

"You called me?" She asked lifting both eyebrow.

"Yeah, a few days ago now I left you a message."

"Sorry but I haven't receive any message from you." She lied. She had unfinished business which she had no desire what so ever to discus on her big day. "But how did you get my number in the first place?"

"I have my ways of finding out things beside I think we need to talk."

"Talk about what? How you kick me to the crib if so I'm *so* not down for it."
She said standing her ground. He place a hand on her hip.

"Asia, you know it wasn't like that at all."

"But it was like that. Just because your dreams crash and burn don't give you
a reason to think that we could start back were we ended." Her eyes never leaving his
before he speak another word she cut him off. "How about you finish this conversation
with yourself." She proceed to exit the hallway caught his my her left arm.

"Asia please I made a mistake back then. I been a fool for letting you go. Is
that what ya wanna heard me say goddammit I've say it." He said with concern in his
eyes.

"Fool you is you broke my heart I'll never consider putting my heart in harms
way ever again. So could you please let go of my arm Manual Parker before I scream."
She said they stare at each other for a few second then he release her then she walked
away leaving him standing looking at her back with a dump founded expression on his
face.

"Brenda, this town could use a little more spicy even though fine ass R. Kelly
lives here doesn't make it spicy enough for me." Brandon said disguising glare on his
face as he stare at unattractive dude which was staring back licking his lips at him.
"Somebody save me from the ugly trade."

"What is a trade?" Brenda asked Brandon wondering what she was talking
as looked around the room.

"Brenda, you really don't be around that many gay guys have you? Trade just another word for guys on the down low. Check out old boy at four o'clock. Every five second he looks this way at me then lick his lips but not in a noticeable that his wife won't caught him." He said taking his eyes off her returning them back on the guy that was flirting with him.

"Oh my gosh he didn't just do that shit around his wife. It just prove one thing that a man can't be secretive bout their self."

"Feel you on that one but think god I don't share that problem. Khalid treats me like angel there ain't shit he wouldn't do for me. Right now he's working he'll call me when he get off in little bit." He said in a cocky tone truly confident that Khalid wouldn't cheat on him.

"How can you be so sure he hasn't cheated on you before? I don't mean to try to get in your head cause that is your man and you must stand on his words." She said folding her arms to her chest looking around the room then back at him meeting eye contact.

"I don't but if he does I'll know cause his body language tells me if he is cheating on me. He better never in his life cheats on me he'll find out ridiculous I could be." He said rising his voice a tap bit from normal from the look in Brenda eyes she knew without a doubt there was more to Brandon ego.

Before she could respond her cellphone ranged. She went to searching in her purse then picked it out of a hidden pocket then answer waving a finger at Brandon letting him know she'll be on a minute or so. He left her there so she could have her privacy. As he made back into the house his connected with non other than Manual Parker. *Lord, please don't let Asia run into him. Why is he here of all places in Chicago in this city.*

"What up Boe?" Manual said wearing a pleasant smile on his face.

Brandon seem very disguised being in the same room with him and wasn't afraid to show it placing a hand on right hip. "What the fuck are you doing here?"

"I could go where ever I wanna go it's a free country." He said nonchalance was his personalty which like college.

"You know what I mean Manual. Your not welcome here and I could second that. Playa you lost your chance with Asia. She don't want your fucked up ass no more if so I'll slap the shit out of her. I don't understand why she stay with your good for nothing ass." He spoke loud enough to get his point across.

"A nigga could say the same thing after seeing Keith whip your ass a few time." He said giggling tilting his head slightly to the left.

"I bet he wished he never met me cause he ain't here beat me right now motherfucker. Keep testing me I'll put your name on my list." He said confidently knowing what he just said aloud.

"What your saying you took him out?" He laugh. "You too scared to do some shit like that. He said jump and you asked how high."

"Keep playing but I know your secret." Brandon said in a cocky tone.

"I don't have any secrets." He said still laughing.

"You still telling those tails. What a joke? Sweetie, I knew about you slinging that cocaine and you been Keith runner back in college. Oh you didn't thought you were slick and nobody knew about it but I do." Brandon wanted to laugh when Manual expression change into unpleasant glare. *You feel jumpy then jump bitch. There ain't nothing but space over here.* Instead of saying anything he just walked away with his tail between his leg. He could feel Brenda coming up behind him staring in the same direction.

"Was that Manual Parker?" She asked not sure what her eyes was seeing.

"Hell yeah that was that bitch ass nigga." He said looking at her square in the face knowing what was going though her mind.

"Didn't know that he was all that." She said with concern in her eyes. "Hook me up."

"Guess you forgot the part bout him being your girl ex?" He asked knowing the answer to the question already.

"Forgot that part."

"What the rule not to break part?"

"What rule are you talking about?"

"Don't date a friends ex that rule." Brandon said shaking his head at her.

"He's on the down low ain't he?"

"No. at least I don't think."

"*What*? Asia never told me about that." Brenda asked wanting to know more about Manual and Asia past.

"Girl, that's a long story and I do mean long story which don't need to be bought up anymore okay. I don't even feel like rehashing a fucked up situation. Let chat about something else before Asia hears you." Brandon glance in the direction of Asia was approaching from.

"What's good with you two?" Asia said with a suspicious glare when she sudden stop in front of them.

"Is there something you need to tell me?" Brenda asked lifting an brow. Wondering to herself why her best friend of four years the dash bout her relationship with Manual.

"Tell you what?" Asia asked then suddenly it hit her that Manual was there and only Brandon knew they was were an item. "Oh, my bad have you seen him? Look this isn't the time nor the place to be chatting about Manual so could we talk about this later?" Asia facial changed then she quickly walk away not even say a word to either of them.

"Excuse me." Brenda said sucking her teeth.

"I knew she would've been blow about that nigga." Brandon said wearing smirk on his face as he fold his arms tightly to his chest. There was a time in his life that he believed that Manual and Asia was a perfect couple till Manual flaws begin to rinse to the surface. It was then he realize that true love was just a fairytale that should stay in books on shelves.

Rocsat at the bar not too long from his apartment hanging out with Zeus and his co-worker Phillip Allen. It was actually his first time out in a while. He spent his days working none stop for the simple reason that he was disturb by the let down he had with Asia. He wanted a relationship for a very long time to express how badly he wanted her. To be rejected in the end the way he did left him feeling so defended which was the second time in the year he felt that way over a woman.

Phillip lean in over so that he could hear him over the music. " What's egging you man cause you been bugging for a while now."

He shrugged his shoulders. "Ain't nothing wrong with me bruh."

"Shit he just tripping over Asia that's all. Man I told you to go and tell her how you feel. Cuzzo, you really starting to get on my fucking nerves man for real." Zeus said with a grin.

"Who is she?" Phillip said wondering who the female was and why her name never came up before now.

"Nobody." Rocsaid not wanting to talk about it any longer.

"Sure she not. Man, Phillip she has been his college home girl who he finally banged for the first time but now she don't want it to happen again." Zeus said telling all Rocbusiness to anyone who would listen to him. Rocsurely wasn't amused by his action.

"Trust me it's gonna happen again." Phillip said with a grin.

"No it's not I saw that look in her eyes then I knew she meant it." Rocshot back at Phillip convinced that it never happen again.

"How can you be so sure cause it happen to me a few years back and now were married if you play your cards right it just might be your tail too." Phillip confess to the both of them. "Just prove to her that you feeling her then she'll reveal how she feels for you."

"I hope your right about that cause I don't think I gonna be around for long stay tune and see." He meant very word that came out his mouth. He wasn't the type to just to sat and wait on anyone specially on a woman attention. Looking past Phillip shoulder he spotted his victim for the night to ease in pain. Rising off the stool he excuse himself as he proceed to make his played his cards right his manhood depended on it. "What up shawty?"

"I don't think that matter." She said looking back at her girl friend then begin talking once more like he never approached her at all then she felt his present sit there looking back up at him. "You still here?"

"Yeah I am and I'm not leaving till we have a conversation of our own. So how about you tell me your name." He said looking directly into her eyes.

"Your memory not good at all. Jennifer, girl get this he don't remember me and was staring at my phat ass and all." She said looking back at her home girl then back at him. " That your people Zeus am I right?"

He glare at her real hard trying to figure out who this woman was then like a light bulb came on inside his head as it was crystal clear. "I thought you looked familiar to me. Candy right?" He said grinned uncontrollably.

"Yeah you got it right that's my name." She said with nonchalance rolling her eyes not really wanting to talk to him anymore.

"I notice you have no drinking can I buy you a drink?" He said winking his left eye at her wearing a light smile.

"You know what after this long crazy ass day I had sure why not a drink a club soda please and thank you Rocthat very kind of you." She said with pleasant tone graceful that he asked.

"Yo Jennifer you want anything to drink?" He asked her friend not leaving her out just because it is the proper thing to do. She accepted his offer she told him what she wanted then he left and came back a few minutes later once he pass them their drinks they begin talking again. After chatting for a while Zeus and Phillip join them till they had to leave to be with their wives. He and Candy exchange numbers among each other.

He open his front door and felt the present of Asia all over again. Reaching for cellphone searching though his contact for an name when he found it he called.

"Hello." A female said softly.

"It's me Roc ."

"Rocwho?"

"You just gave me this number earlier at the bar tonight." He explained.

"I ain't been to a bar tonight. I'm sorry sir you have the wrong number." She said.

"Sorry she must have gave me the wrong number. I'm sorry I bothered you ma'am." He said feeling disappointed.

"RocI'm just fucking with you. I knew who you were caller I.D silly." She bust out laughing.

He started to smile feeling relief from being rejected. "You got jokes but I'll get you back when you least expect it wait and see."

"Oh, you piloting on me now. Rocthat isn't a good move at all." She said still laughing till a tear came out of her right eye. "I bout to take a shower. Thank you for the drink lately life been really ruff. Sorry if it's seem as if I was dissing you cause it wasn't that way at all."

"I didn't took it that way at all." He lied to her cause he cause he did took it on a personal level plus his ego was busied which it take a lot to get to him. "How about dinner tomorrow night?"

"Let me get back to you on that about it." She paused for a brief second then reply. "Yeah, I am free after a meeting which suppose to end at about five thirty."

"I'll pick you at you placed." He said.

"I'll met you there. When I'm ready for you to come to my place you will be invited. You see I just met you. You could be a masked murder or something." She joked.

"Cool with me but I did wanted to surprise you. How about I text you the address were meet up there." He said in a hopeful tone.

"Okay, you text me but I really need to take this shower." She said in a rushy tone. They said their goodbyes to each other then they disconnected there conversation.

"Who was that on the phone?" A male voice said.

"Our plan is just getting started I told you it was gonna work the way I said it was gonna work." She said wearing a smirk on her face.

"Your plan could sometime back fire then you be looking like a stupid jackass. From here on out follow my plan then everything be on track just the way I need it to be on my time line the way it should be." He said glaring in deep into her eyes wondering what was going thought her mind.

"Okay, okay, okay I get your point. So claim your nerves cause I don't take idol threats and shit from no fucking nobody." She shouted across the room to him.

"Look here bitch I never made an idol threat in my motherfucking life so don't make me find somebody else to do the job." He said with a dead look in his eyes.

"Okay I said I'll do the job." She said.

"You better do the job. I'll be in touch with ya." He said then he turn his body around exiting the room leaving her alone nerviness begin to take over on her. The only thing she could do was stand rocking herself as tears of fear rolled down her eyes.

For the past two days Asia been tripping over Manual so much that it caused her to get a headache. She knew he it was on purpose that he showed up at her open house since then he'd called her home phone leaving message after message at least twice a day she need clarity and fast picking up her phone she dialed a number which she haven't dialed in while.

"What up?" Rocsay in a up beat tone.

"Hi, I need a man point of view on this situation I got going on." She said with a tear dropping from her left eye.

"Shot." He says with a nonchalance in tone of voice.

"I mean if I called at a bad time just tell me cause your sounding like there a problem with me calling you." She snapped at him.

"You good." He said in a not convincing tone.

"Anyway a few weeks ago I seen somebody. While not anybody Manual Parker. He show up at my open house about two weeks ago and trust me we had words. When he left he left me in a twisted mood. For the past two days he's been calling me non stop tryina get another chance with me. I really don't know what to do. Roc , what should I do?" She plead into the phone.

He didn't say a word for a brief minute searching words to begin. "Wow, maybe you should have dinner with him and resolve the issue at hand. You been holding on to him for years comparing other guys to him."

"It's not even like that besides I don't feel like I can trust myself alone with him. After how he did me."

"You could handle yourself just fine. I seen you in action plenty of times over the years so I know you could handle it." He said trying to convince her and himself.

"Manual, was always hard to talk to I can't do that Roc ."

"Be brave face your fears, face him it'll help you properly make you feel better and him in the process too."

"Maybe okay I'll think about it then I'll make my vote on what I should do. How you been doing anyway?" She said changing the subject.

"I'm fine had a date the other night which went completely well. We suppose to be hooking up tonight." He said with excitement in his voice for the first time in there conversation.

"Well how was the sex cause I know you done hit it?"

"Actually we haven't had sex yet I didn't want to I'm starting a new thing. I want it to be a good relationship compare to others."

"Oh, that's really good. So what's her name?" Asia asked.

"Candy."

"Nice let me guess she like candy?" Asia joked.

"It means_" He said with a attitude.

"Candace I know. You knew that Roc . You really needs to lighten up because your being a sour pussy. Ever since the other day when we you know. You been dissing me like hell."

"Shit Asia, your the one been dissing me I been calling you *days* and then you fucking say it was a *mistake*. I have real feeling for you but you don't give a *fuck*." Rocsnapped hard not thinking about what he was saying.

"What do you want me to say it just fucking happen I was embarrassed by the situation and needed time to think. Beside I see how you act with the others girls.

You just run though them the way you do. I ain't nobody toy or a game lets be for real Rocabout this you know how you really is. Do you expect me to be one of the those chick?" She shout though the phone waiting for his response to her question. She knew it wouldn't long at all.

"FUCK YOU ASIA." He yelled.

"Well you already did that shit and that shit will never happen again. See I knew it was a mistake. All those other bitches you done dogged out and you can't take it yourself. Huh," She said then hanged up in his face before he had a choice to respond. Walking into the bedroom taking off her shoes first then her jogging and under garments. Getting into the shower only thing she could think of was Rocand how it was a mistake to be drinking then going home with him. When she was drying off her hair in the bathroom in front of the mirror the house phone ranged causing her to rush over to answer not really wanting to be bothered. "What the hell do you want?" She answered ignoring the caller I.D.

"You ain't gotta talk to me like that on the phone cause I ain't done shit to you." Brenda snapped back at Asia.

"My bad I thought you were somebody else. What's good?" She murmured.

"Ain't nothing I been busy with Nay Nay that I haven't been chilling with you in a few days so you wanna have lunch later?" Brenda murmured.

"I gotta show a house across town but after that I'm free till three." She said with the displeased expression that didn't hide it's self from her lips.

"How about our spot?"

"Sure."

"You think Brandon wanna to join us?" She asked.

"Don't know but I'll ask him once I get off the phone with you. I'll see you about twelve thirty is that good with you?"

"Yea, that will be fine. But really I need to get dress and head out. I'll see you later at the spot." She said before hanging up.

Brenda sat with her legs crossed in deep thought when Asia walked in. It wasn't till she sat down in the chair next to her. "It most be something deep weighting on you do you wanna talk about it?" Was the first thing that came out of her mouth.

She shrugged her shoulders with a puzzled look on her face. "No, nothing wrong with me. Sorry but Boe won't be showing up he said that he had plans that he couldn't get out of."

"Oh damn then he just have to catch up later whenever that is so tell me what's the deal with him."

"What you mean?" Asia said in jokey tone.

"Don't get me wrong he seem to be a cool guy and all but he might have a dark side you need to worry about."

"Dark side." She repeat with a slight smile. "I don't understand what your talking about."

Brenda looked directly in her eyes then back outside then back at her. "I mean he went to a place that I've never seen him go first he was happy the next thing I knew he turn to devilish version of himself. Ever since he started chatting with Manual he's been another person. Did those two had bad blood back when you all was in college or something?"

Asia was about speak but the waitress arrived with two trays one with buffalo wings and fries the other had fried shrimps and fries. She didn't leave till she place their drinks in front of them. Asia take a sip of her coke first.

"So are you gonna answer my question or do I need to repeat myself Asia, cause you know I don't have a problem with it." Brenda stated.

"Sorry what did you say again?" Asia said then remember what Brenda said before the waitress showed up again. "Oh yeah now I remember. Back in college Brandon's first love in college Kieth and Manual hang together that how Brandon and I meet then start becoming real good friends. Kieth treated him like shit. He used to have bruises on his shoulder even though he deny it I knew Kieth was beating up on him. I wonder why sometimes he never left him till one day Manual came home told me about what had happen to Kieth I knew that Brandon fucked him up."

Brenda look complete surprised expression on her face learning what she learned about Brandon past. "But that don't explain anything about why he and Manual Parker don't get along with each other."

"Well, they never really did saw eye to eye. Never really figure that part out yet." Asia confess. "So how your doing other than worrying about Brandon?"

"Everything is everything with me and Nay Nay she so thrilled about her play she's going to be in and I just know she'll do the damn thing."

"I know she will because I seen her in action over a week ago the last time I was over there." Asia said with a smile thinking about Brenda's daughter.

Brenda smile suddenly faded before Asia could say what's wrong she begin speaking. "We been friends for the last four years or so right?"

Asia nodded her letting her know she understood what she said then her mind begin to wonder what is she getting at?

"We tell each other everything right?" She asked but Asia respond to her question she cute her off. "So why you never mention to me that you use to date him? I knew you knew him."

"Cause it was something I didn't want to talk about for a reason he broke my heart. I thought I wouldn't see him again."

"But you didn't have to hide him from me of all people." She snapped.

"Actually, I planned on talking to you about Manual today before we part ways because he's been calling and I don't know how to handle it. I tried talking about this to Rocbut that nigga is tripping real hard as a fuck and Boe's busy handling business with his man and shit so that just leaves you."

"Why do I have to be your last option?" She said sounding offended rolling her eyes back Asia like she got a problem with her.

"It's not even like that so stop bugging out about this Brenda. If your baby daddy was to do some fucked up shit like to you in the past what would you if he comes back in the picture trying get back with you. Would you get over that?" Asia ask with concern in her eyes wondering what was about to come out Brenda mouth.

She thought for a second as though she was she searching for the right words. "Truthfully, I think you should meet up with him and see what he wanna say to him. You two do have unfinished business to deal with so face them while your ready."

Looking out the window for a brief second then looked back at Brenda pondering, searching for the right words and then it hit her like she never got closure. A part of her wondered about there unsolved history when she thought bout that a rage took over her. She reached in her purse pulling out her cellphone then begin to search for a name then press the call button after the first ring he picked up. "What up short cake? I'm glad you called me."

"Little surprised myself to be honest with you. You keep calling me like a fucking clown so I guess I had to call you back. At least once." She said rolling her eyes at Brenda who placed a smile on her face. "What are you doing tomorrow night?"

"Yo nothing good ma, how bout eight o'clock at your favorite restaurant on the south side of town. Is that cool with you?"

"That's fine I guess." She said unsure of the whole situation. "Okay then I'll see you then. Bye." Then she hung up. "Girl I hope your happy now."

"I'm happy when you get a man."

"I get one when I get one so chill. Gotta show a house on the mid east I'm a call you later and then we're finish this conversation later. Okay." As she gather her things.

"Girl that's cool with me cause I gotta pick baby girl from school early for her doctor appointment at three." She said with a smile as she reached in her purse pulling out twenty dollars then placing it on the table as she raised to her feet then begin walking along side Asia. "Then we could talk about what your gonna wear. How your gonna do your hair?"

"Plan on wearing it up he usually like it that way for some odd reason. It's a guy thing so don't even think about asking me a thing about it." She said a quick glance before opening up the door to let her though first then herself. Brenda didn't respond after almost a minute of silents they said there goodbyes then went there separate ways.

Asia stepped out of her 2009 Lexus rushing into her town house she suddenly stop in her tracks when she saw Roc standing with his arms fold staring back at her. She begin to walk in a fast paste temping to walk pass him when he grabbed her by her left arm snatched her back to him real quick. "What the fuck are you doing here? And get your those paws off me." She yelled with anger in her eyes.

"Why you bugging Asia acting like it didn't happen and like you don't remember shit bout that night." He said glaring at her.

"I think we said what we had to say to each other earlier so if you don't mind I'm heading in here to relax my nerve for the rest of the night thank you and bye." She snatched away him hard rolling her eyes.

"We need to get this all over with."

"Get over what I thought we were over this a few weeks ago but you keep bring it up I'm getting tired of this. Say what you got to say then leave as you came."

"See this is why I don't get into relationship with female like you. You knew for years I wanted a relationship with you but when something happen you run like a little girl."

"First off all you sleep with the more than the same amount of bitches as to appose to the many times you changes your shoes in a week so the question is why would I fuck around get myself in a fucked up situation with you and those other hoes. In fact I know you already start dating somebody already. In fact you told me so." She said with a fake smile. He didn't respond in stand he just storm off to his car then he was gone. She knew without a doubt in her mind that he was already dating some else that was topical Roc can't have what he wants so he runs to the next thing.

Brandon has been out of contact with Asia and his new found friend Brenda for a minute but he made his best effort into being there on time as usual. From the corner of his eyes he saw Asia coming up along side her was Brenda. He gave them a slight smile then looked back the stage which done started. They didn't speak til after the play ended as they waited for Brenda to return with her little girl. "Can't stay long got plans an later on."

"I guess you too busy for ya girl thinking your all that and then some cause you got a chocolate brother at home don't mean a thing to me." She murmured with a slight smile.

Brandon just smile from ear to ear he knew she was joking with him. The sound of loud children running all over the place and their parents chasing them around close to his side before he accidentally hit one of the little children wasn't the mood to pass words with anyone. "Don't play Asia besides he handling business and I got business of my own thank you very much. We suppose to be meeting up in after while. Everything been going smoothly lately I just wish he didn't have to go out of town so much."

"Why he always traveling?"

"He's a contractor that handle major business all over the United States and sometimes over seas. Asia, why you all in my ass and shit." He said as he fold his arms tightly to his chest.

"Oh for real?"

"No girl for play play. Before you even try to get mad set yourself up for that. Where is Brenda and her little angel at?" He said looking around the entrance for them.

"You so picking blind that you can't even see them twenty feet away from your silly ass self." She said looking over his shoulders at Brenda and her little girl.

"Oh, there you go I been looking for you for far too long." Brandon said rolling his eyes giving her a quick chuckle. "Asia and I been waiting to see you little Arnazejah to tell her how proud we are in her performance."

"You rocked it like no other." Asia added.

"Thank you so much Mr. Brandon and Auntie Asia." Arnazejah said with sparkles in her eyes there was no doubt that she did amazing job. "I had so much fun can't wait til next time."

"Yea, my baby blew me away. I almost yelled out that's my baby up there but I didn't want to be too ghetto." She admitted.

"You need to stop cause half of the people in the room could hear you and I pretend like I didn't know who was in matter of fact what your name." Brandon said sizing Brenda up and down. *Who was she fooling the only ghetto female I hear in there.*

"You better be glad my baby is here otherwise I'll handle you my way." She said cutting her eyes at him.

"Whatever you'll get handle is more like it." He sucked his teeth then looked at his watch which was on left waist. "Why my man haven't text me yet he knows how pissed I could get bout_"

"Stuff like this. Brandon don't forget where you is. Children in our presence lets not forget that. That's properly why that man of yours have issues with you now." Asia cut him off giving him a sharp look.

"Whatever Asia, you don't even know what I was about to say so your tail need to stop finishing my sentence before I put you in check." He said low enough for to her and Brenda to hear what he had to say. That was something he couldn't stand was to be cut in a middle of his sentence Khalid had to find out the hard way he is a force to be reckon with. Bringing a fake smile to his face realizing that Arnazejah was in his presence. "So did you enjoy yourself lil one?" He said playfully to the eight year old girl.

"Stupid thought I just said I had fun. Are you hard at hearing or something." Arnazejah said with a ignored expression on her face shaking her head from side to side.

"You gone leave my baby alone. And Arnazejah, you better mind you mouth before I beat your behind when we get home. You better mine yourself he is a grown man." Brenda said patting her daughter on the back.

Brandon was about to answer but his cell ranged stopping him in his tracks grabbing his cell out of the case which it was placed quickly pressing the answer button on the screen. "Hey you bout to head to the spot in a few. Baby, wish you had come cause it was the bomb." He chuckle softly as he moved away from Asia, Brenda and her little girl.

"I'm gone have to cancel on our plans tonight honey." Khalid said sharply the sound of stuff moving around in the back.

"*Where the hell you at?*" Brandon said with a attitude placing his left hand on his hip not really paying any attention to the children walking or running pass him.

"Babe, why you always have to question what I'm doing shit you already know what I do for a living. A nigga give you anything you could ever asked for but yet you still have the nerve to bring that foolishness where the hell you are out your mouth." He said with anger in his voice.

"Who the hell you talking to like that Khalid your jumping out of character like a cat searching for a piece of meat in the trash don't make me let you strive to death motherfucker. I must've loosen your pants. Better be glad I love you enough to let this slide." Brandon sucking his teeth.

"You must be tryina show your ass in front your friends cause we both know my pants has always been the way I wanted it to be loosen. Shit, it been that fucking way before I meet your ass. And don't worry a nigga gone give you some dick when a nigga get there so stop crying."

Brandon felt heat begin to rise in his body. Khalid always knew just what to say but he couldn't just let him win that easy he had to play it off. "Ain't nobody crying over some dick fool. I just wanted you and you alone. So when you is coming home?" Brandon said licking his lips making sure their were good and wet.

"When I get there damn honey why you making this so complicated you gone make a nigga fuck you up one of these days." He said teasingly.

Already knowing what that was code for he reacted before Khalid knew what had hit him. "I see you in bout a week. Bye." He said then hang up in his face. Forcing a fake smile on his face walking back towards Asia, Brenda and her lil girl. "Miss anything?"

"What's to miss unless it's your own date with Mr. Perfect canceling on your date." Asia said with a smirk on her face. "Yes we can read your fake smile on your face."

"The world ain't gone end just yet." Brenda said then begin to laugh. "It happens sometimes you gone live to see another day."

"Trust I'm gone be just fine with or without him. So what's the plan for the night?"

"I'm about to take Arnazejah to McDonald's so she could get her a fish meal baby, and then I'm gone call it a night." Brenda said then yawned hard.

"About to a drink with someone in about a hour from now." Asia said looking at Brenda.

Brandon fold his arms tightly to his chest his attitude did a switch cause he already know the answer to who she was going to meet. "I know damn well you ain't going to see that fucked up ass nigga Manuel Parker. Just don't say shit to me if he shit on you again." He said then realized he was standing by Arnazejah. "I'm sorry sweet pea, I didn't mean for you hear that."

"You need to watch your mouth around my baby besides it's her life. Why do you care so much bout her business anyway? Your man should keep your mind twisted." Brenda said.

"I'm a friend and being a real friend I have to express how I feel bout this situation at hand, you don't know nothing bout this at all so whatever. People these days needs to mind there own business cause they be making themselves look stupid on so many levels." He said placing his right hand on his hip glaring his eyes hard at her. Brenda didn't say a word instead she grabbed Arnazejah hand walking away without saying a word.

"Why the hell did you talk to her like that? She's my friend and you need to respect Brenda or our friendship is gonna have a major problem." Asia snap looking him straight in his eyes before he could say another word she continue. "And second of all if I could have a drink with Manuel Parker. I'm gonna have a drink goddamn drink with Manuel Parker. Brenda was right it was none of your business nor yous place. We friends but don't use or abuse our friendship."

Brandon cleared his throat looked around the room. It wasn't Brenda that pissed him off it was the fact Khalid had tried his nerves. "You know what your right I should let a man get to me and neither should you. Asia shouldn't go though what I endure a lot pain dealing with Keith and Jermaine. Keith really messed up my reality and reality bites do hurts. To be truthful you chose the road you take carefully cause there is repercussion in everything you do Asia."

"Sounds like you been though something deep care in the past that don't mean it'll happen to me." Asia said. "And who is this Jermaine you never told me the tale of him only person I know about was Kieth who I glad you left and Khalid but never Jermaine."

"And you won't hear and ever hear bout that bastard ever." He said in claim voice then looked at his watch. *Wouldn't know where to start on the the subject of Jermaine. I mean where do I begin anyway.* He thought to himself. "Well it's getting late so I'll call you later on in the afternoon. Asia, I just hope you know what doing."

"I do Boe so stop worrying about me cause I'm gonna be just fine." Asia said before they parted ways in opposite direction. She didn't need a soul to worry bout her. She could handle herself just fine. As she pulled out the parking lot she wondered to herself *this isn't the Boe she was use to.*

Asia stood behind Manual Parker when she came in he was obvious he was too into a conversation with someone who she could careless about. She wonder why she was there in the first place. They both been though the storms after storm which pull them apart but yet she was there just because he called her. "I'm here." She whisper softly as she grab her seat then placing herself in.

"My bad dimples that was a important phone call. How long were you standing there anyway?" He said with a smile that will make a random woman melt in a second. Those eyes are the same one she loved most about him for a reason he never knew.

"Not long at all just making sure you wasn't talking to another woman." She joked resting her chin on her hand. She wasn't thinking bout nothing just where their conversation would be going. After grinning for a few seconds. "Manual it's nothing like that, you and I both know that your not that type of man unless you change, shit I mean you are famous worth more than a millions of dollars."

"When it comes to you I'll always be faithful with others women maybe." He said with devilish smile.

"How many *women* have there been Manual? Not that I'm being noisy if it makes any difference I only been three for me." Asia said with the quickness she knew her number very well.

"More than that you know I gotta have it on the regular. Look Asia let's cut the bullshit I don't expect you to give a nigga another chance since we both decided to end things. I was a boy tryina love a woman but I'm here hoping to get another chance to make it right." He said sincere.

She had a look like she just left earth for a brief minute. For her it was completely beyond fixable the way they ended their relationship pushed her so far to the edge of insanity that seeing him which she now regretted brought back all the painful memories. She sat straight up in her seat looking at then glance down at the menu. "Aw, what am I gonna eat tonight cuz everything they serve is calling my stomach."

Khalid hung up his cellphone sitting on the edge of the bed staring out into space not to far in the unknown. "Wish he stop with that bullshit a nigga ain't got time for sissy ass shit." He said to another person who stood in the doorway with their back to him obviously listen to them but wasn't talking to the person. "I know you hear me."

They turn around in his direction to see if he was talking to them with they're right hand in they're hair. "Hisham, was you talking to me or yourself?" They said licking they're lips leaning back on the on the door.

"Don't play with me cause you already know." He said with anger in his eyes they knew he wasn't in playing one bit.

"Hisham, you better claim your nerves down ain't no need to mess up my buzz right now. Why the fuck you letting dump fuck fuck up what we got going on. He'll get handle when the time is right and right now the time ain't right one bit. Getting yourself caught up in a twisted situation can do that to you boo don't worry." They murmured softly to Khalid.

"Baby bring that ass on over here for daddy."

"Daddy, can I ride it?" They asked with nothing but pleasure in there eyes taking a step closer to him. "Let me easy your mind of all the confusion from your mind."

"Only you know how to ease the stress for your daddy. You really how to please your man don't you?" He murmured.

They walked over stopping at the foot of the bed on they're hands begin to crawl toward him batting they're eyes. "Do I daddy. This body is all yours and nobody else so you didn't answer my question can I ride it?"

"You already know the answer so just bring it, put that phat ass on like you want it." He said with a smirk on his face. He didn't plan to leave until the next day there was one thing he didn't like and that was to be tried like a little child which was something he never liked in his life.

Chapter Two

About three weeks later...

Asia woke up acking from head to toe stomach feeling like it reading boil over as she straight the bedroom down the hall til she got into the bathroom to her knees leaning over toilet throwing up just about everything she eat the night before when she get out Manuel. When she thought she was done cradle on the bathroom between the toilet and the sink. Tears falling from her eyes wishing she reach her cell so she could call Brenda or somebody anybody at this as she begin to move her mouth started water she knew more was about pour as she lean over the toilet just time.

She had to show a house at ten o'clock from the looks of it she wouldn't be able. Manage to get to her bedroom laying on the bed with the phone in her left hand as she us her right hand to call her leaving a messages boss answering machine pressing the end button before she could drop it beside her on the bed the cell phone instantly startling her. She answer with a painful "Hello."

"Morning beautiful lady." Manuel says in his deep voice.

At this point she didn't want to be bother by anybody as she use her left hand to massage her belly hoping to claim the pain. "This isn't a good time Parker. I'm not feeling well at all."

"I'm on my way over there and I am not taking no for a answer."

"You had a interview I don't want to mess that up for you. I mean that could be a chance of a lifetime." She tried her best to get him to go to his interview.

"You is way more important than some damn interview. I be there in bout thirty minutes. Is there anything you need before I get there." He asked.

She thought his words were sweet but she knew trying to get him change his decision was out of the question so he let him know that she needed some soup and orange juice before they both hung up. She picked herself off of the bed dragging herself down finally she'd the front door unlocking it then walking to the nearest sofa where she fall to sleep almost immediately.

Brandon stood in front of Brenda door nervously waiting on her to come out side to take Arnazejah to school. Not even wanting to ring the bell for the simple fact that he wanted to surprise her when she open her door surprise she was. For a brief moment neither one of then bother to speak til Arnazejah broke the silence. "Hi Mr. B, nice to see you again."

He wear a bright smile on his face when glanced in the direction of the little girl. "Hello little one I missed you and your mom so much." He glancing back up her Brenda.

"Could have fooled me." She blurred out turning her back the front door then grabbing her left hand was they proceed pass him.

"Look I could be butt head sometimes for that I'm apology. I need to talk to somebody which that is you. I'll walk with you or you want me to take you and my Arnazjah to the school house." Brandon said with a sincere smile on his face she return slight smile.

"Nigga, you better offer me and mine a ride. Showing up in that nice ass car." She said.

"Yea, you better take." Arnazjah as she marched over toward Brandon BMW pulling the door open once open climbing on the backseat. "Momma you better hurry before Mr. B change his mind."

"He better not if he know what's good for him. Baby, he don't wanna get cut." Brenda as she walked pass him as him follow right behind her.

Brenda most of the day with Brandon even though he didn't talked about what was obviously rocking his nerves which was puzzling her to no end. With all her might she tried not to bring what to the surface. As they walked along the lake side in the park Brandon seem so intertwine with nature that took him off guild when she asked the obvious question. "Did you brought me out here talk about whats really bothering you?"

"Whatcha talking bout?" Brandon said looking puzzle.

"You said earlier bout you got stuff on your mind and that you need tell somebody which that would be me." She explain what he told her but not quit the way he said it before but close hey he got the picture where she was coming from.

At first he didn't speak as if he were searching the right words to come out then looked out in space. "I love him so much still can't believe he's cheating on me after all I've done for that motherfucker. Brenda I ain't seen him bout two weeks. Guess my cookies ain't no good for him no more damn, he's my everything."

"Are you sure he is cheating cause when you assume you end up looking real stupid." She said placing a hand on his shoulder caress him as he continue to look out in space. "You need to talk to him and find out the truth there more than one reason for a man to act the way he does. Hey you should have figure that part out ain't you one of them." She giggle.

"Sometimes you just know when a nigga acting shady." He rolled his eyes still not looking in her direction. "Ain't shit I could do bout it. Ride or die that's what I gotta do."

"Okay, so what hell your gonna do bout it? You know I got your sadiddy ass back. Shit you be getting on my got damn nerves make a bitch wanna fuck you." She murmured.

"I'm thinking bout a change of look what you think?" He said annoy her last remake turn his eye contact back to her for the first time in a while wearing light smile. "What you think about me cutting my hair?"

"Look your a man ain't it?" She asked sarcastically know his answer. "Of course you should cut all that damn hair off you head."

"Whatever." He said rolling his eyes at her. "I am not hair, it makes me who I am. Brenda don't be a hatter all your life, green don't look good on you"

"You is imitation fish I'm the real pussy. Ask a man and he'll tell you this some shit between." She said shaking her head from side to side. They both burst into laughter

Manuel showed up with the things Asia asked for and then some. After putting bags groceries in the kitchen he came back in the living room leaning over Asia who was asleep picking her up off the the sofa and carrying her down the hallway to her bedroom laying in her bed for a minute he stood there watching her. To him she looked like angel. She cracked her eyes just enough to see him staring at her murmured softly to him. "You could be a good man but still can't believe the one time I needed you most you chosed your football career over us. Manuel how do you expect me to forgive you after that shit?" A tear begin form in her left eye.

"I don't know how you could but we can be the way we were before. Asia your my heart my everything if I could change the past baby you know I would." Manuel said sincerely.

"It would never be the same after seeing what be like. Your a fucking bastard Manuel Parker. Your the reason I'm still single a part of me hates your fucking gusts. If you hadn't done what you did..." She caught herself. "Can you bring me some chicken noodle soup. Thanks." She said as she moved over in the opposite direction not wanting to face him for another minute. He that as the sign to leave her alone for a while he felt she needed and so did.

"Yeah baby." Brandon said with excitement in his eyes as he stare in the mirror at the beauty salon. His hair was cut to inches off his should. Having weird feel coming him. "A Ross, could you throw some tiny curls cute like *Hally Berry*?"

Ross was beautician that was doing his doe since he arrived who at first believed his hair was weave till he played though it for about three to five minutes then he finally believe me. *Dump ass* He thought to himself. "I wish you ain't had me cut that pretty hair of yours. I'm tryina figure out why in the hell you doing this shit. Ain't no fucking man gonna make me cut out all my hair *hell* to the *no*." He yelled shaking his head still couldn't deal with the fact that I've decided to cut off my hair.

"Well, he didn't make me do shit Ross, it's called a new attitude and that's what this is." Brandon said smirk across his face.

Brenda stood there with a shock expression written across her face. "Looking more like a man by the minute in fact you should have all that motherfucker off asap. Stop tryina look like a woman cause in the end you'll still be imitation crab meat." laughing hilariously.

"He, he hell *Ms. Thang*. Don't cause we please a man better than you can." Ross sarcastically then rolled his eyes so hard it looked like he might have gain a headache in the process.

"Okay, man loves his self some me always have always will Big Momma. He said he a man is better to deal with a woman it's complicated. We respect each boundaries." Brandon said still glaring at himself in the mirror. "Brenda, shut the fuck up you stay talking shit about shit. You just a hater."

"You ain't shit for me to hate on." Brenda spit back him, he give her a responds other than him sucking his teeth.

Later that day after taking Brenda to pick up her little girl up from school then dropped them off at her place. On the ride home thinking about Khalid expression on his face Brandon knew how happy he have been to see his new hair do. Later home cleaning the living room he could hear a key going though the deadbolt lock knowing the only person it was Khalid he'd rush over to the front door to greet him when the door open was looking at the keys in his hands but when he finally glanced in Brandon direction his smiled turn into a frown for a minute he remain silence then he spoke. "What the fuck did you do to your damn hair?"

"*What* it look like Khalid I cut my fucking hair, motherfucker watch your damn mouth when you talk to me. You got got some serious issues and need to put them in check."

"No your the one with the issues. You must've forgot what you ***promise*** me."

"Forget what promise your talkin bout Khalid?" Brandon said thought for a split second this motherfucker is getting off the topic of the evening. At this point he didn't give a damn about a promise I've might have made to this nigga. "Who the damn the trick you messin with cause I know you too well?"

"I ain't fuckin nobody but you, beside I would been left you. I know one you better fix that hair issue before I fuck you up in here." He said turning back to him when he said. "In fact put some braids in that bitch and you got to next week." Slamming the bedroom door so hard that the sound echo in Brandon ears for about three minutes later even then his hands been trembling tears started to rolled down his cheeks. Khalid never speak in that tone with him before.

Interlude take II

Brenda and I left Asia and her unexpected guest in the alone while we converse about current events and such. "I just can't believe that fool bought his tired aspirin up in here." Brenda said with a disgusting on her face.

"You need to give give him a break that has one last chance to get her back before she jumps the broom. I mean you would understand if the shoe was on the other foot."

"*Hell* naw never in my lifetime, if so please slap the hell the out of me for doin that stupid shit. Ugh."

"I thought I was hell best you got me bet." I giggled looking at Brenda like she lost her mind. Instantly my mind wondered to Jermaine who was rumored to been married Kelly who deserved a better man. I felt like a fool for thinking he could change but like saying leopard can't change it's spots.

"Shit you number one Asia before me shit that's why we get along we each other so perfectly well. Shit I was just about to fuck you one." Brenda said then sip her drink while I on the other hand carried a devilish smile thinking of all the bull shit I've done the past and believe I've done some off the chain.

"Fish keep playing with me. Sometimes I think you wish you've lived like do now if so you can't handle what I do on day to day basis. And one more thing please stop profanity in this church."

"Oh snap this wine has got me buzzed my bad but never that. Don't play with me imitation crab meat. I just with I had a man with money so I'll be set for life." She as put her drink to take another sip of drink.

I let the words escaped my lips before I could try to stop them from hitting the air. "Be care what you wish for cause you don't know what it takes to keep him." My nerves begin to bother me something it hadn't since the night of my graduation when I break up with Kieth the way we didn't see coming but I knew it would happen something like that.

"What you mean?" Brenda question brought me back to the situation I put myself in.

"Nothing child, I didn't mean a thing by that but just be careful about whatcha want." I said hoping she'll buy my little white lie.

"You never told me how forgive him for his indiscretion a few years ago. I don't know if I can handle my man cheated on me." She said with her eyes directly at me waiting my response.

"Child, what your talking about?" I said with a shock expression my face.

"You told me that he cheated on you."

"Sh... I mean sweetie he never cheated on me." I said tryina figure out why she think that cause I would tell if he did. I know Khalid from head to toe inside out.

"Stop playing you told me out your own mouth that he cheated own you but you couldn't prove it." Brenda claim.

"Must be somebody that look like me." I said wondering how we got on this subject in the first place but she kept on being noisy so I decided to let my eyes roam the room. A familiar face caught my attention she was standing in the far doorway but not too noticeable but she was giving me a mean mug so I did what do block her out of my circle so I get back in this conversation with Brenda which was still dead set on talking about a time Khalid allegedly had some kind of affair on me. I did my best switch this in another direction and fast. So used my left hand to playful twirl some of my hair wearing my condescending smile. "Oh, child ain't nobody got time to be thinking bout that foolishness your trying to disguise is that all you wanna yap?" Returning my eyes back to the far door but she done disappear for the moment and I was glad for that.

Brenda seem like she catch my drift cause she change the subject with the quickness. "How long did you think he needed to chat with and do you still the wedding is on?"

I didn't know for sure but when it came to having two different men both with big pocket I knew she had a win win situation I was proud to her my girl. "I don't know but I hate to waste sexy outfit on a day full of promises." I blurted out while I was speaking text message came through on my cell.

"Mr. Steele came you meet in the hallway asap. We have business to disguise and I feel like this should be face to face."

I couldn't do a thing but blushing uncontrollably as heat starts to rise. My true emotion hasn't yet to show up on my face. Brenda looked at me like it was Khalid was texted me but it wasn't. "Sorry Brenda I make a important phone call." I murmured as I begin to stand to my feet then headed toward the before she could say a word to me. As I entered through the doubled door I could see the same female who was mean mug me like she lost her picking mind maybe she did. "So do I know you and how you got my number Ms.?"

"I know you like to role play personally I don't give-" She spit at me but I cut her off before she'd use profanity in the church.

"Ms. your the one tryina role play on me cause I don't know or have a clue to who you are. Please don't make me repeat my first statement." I demanded.

"Where is it Mr. Steele?" She said annoying my question.

"I make have to take the foolishness outside cause your pissing me off. And where is what your talking about?" I said with a puzzle look on my face.

"My package you promise me." She raising her voice a tap bite no one still couldn't hear her at this point.

"What package? We know let take this outside for real."

"NO you need to let me know when you plan to hand my package over." She demanded.

"Huh, child I don't know what ya talking bout. I don't know shi... I mean nothing bout what your talking about." I said turning my back to her heading towards to the nearest exit which wasn't nothing but less than ten feet away she follow behind me closely.

"Mr. Steele stop playing where is it?" She said once they were outside and I'd stop walking a few feet outside of the church before I could turn around to face her by then my whole demeanor change in my face especially in my eyes.

When I finally turn around to face her I almost lost complete. "Darling, I think it's time for you to leave like now before I say something that might hurt your feeling."

She didn't blink as she press her lips together. "You could never hurt my feeling Mr. Steele. Should march in there and everybody your little secret. Trust me I'll do it."

"Bitch, I'll fuck you up if you try and fuck with me. I got what you want so go on make this a day to remember for the rest of your life and you don't wanna live with regret do you sweetie." I said wearing a devilish smile folding my loosely to my chest. She immediately walked away without saying a word as tears fall from her eyes. As she went one way I walked back into the building dropping my arm to my side I didn't stop til I reached a restroom splashing a little water in my face.

"Having fun too much fun I see." A familiar voice said says to me while my eyes were closed coming out a stile right behind me. This day ain't gone get any better I thought to myself grabbing a paper towel drying my face.

I replied. "How so?" Not even looking in their direction while was still drying my face. I was begin to think this day wasn't going to get better but instead interesting by the minute.

"I want my man back." He says placing left hand on his hip starring at me but I couldn't see him cause my back was to him and I was drying my face.

"You may have had once but I got him all the time dear. I paid you to a job and that's all it was a J-O-B. I knew you were a weak bitch and what do weak bitches do fall so easily on the job. Don't get it twisted he was never yours but he was and still my

man. You better get my left overs cause this is man and plan to keep it that was till the

day one of us die." I said using right hand to play in my hair showing off my Gucci watch

slowly turning around to face him putting on my devilish smile back on forgetting I was

in a church.

"I hate you. Always got to have it your way like your at McDonald's or

something this gonna end today on my terms." He says trying to handle me like this way

the streets or something.

"Oh really you think you got me beat? Well we need to tell him everything

and let him decide what he wants." I said looking at the other person. "You should have

took the money I give you and run to start your new life."

"Khalid is my life. I love him with all my heart more than you could ever."

I said nothing for a minute the wedding was on the top of my list then this

girl came up now I have this situation all in one day something had to give. This time I

just might not win this battle. I knew what I sign up for the day I decided to leave Kieth

the way I did. I plan on living to the fullest ride or die. I open my mouth to speak before

a word came out he slap me so hard that he could have been hear halfway down the

hall. I murmured a sentences strong so it rocked his nerves. "The mirror may look like

me wear my clothes sleep with my man a little bite of the time. Don't mean you could

ever be me. There is and always will be only one Brandon Omar Edwards and that

motherfucker ain't no weak bitch like you. Matter of fact you even hit like a bitch. I'll

text you the time for us to handle this matter." It felt like I didn't feel a single thing at all

turn my face back towards the man looking identical like myself but not so much

completely like me there was marks on one our body that separating us apart.

Almost six years ago...

After I left Keith on that floor that night I went on a mission to change my life

for the better good. I enrolled into college in Alabama. I wanted to pursue acting class as

a child I've always wanted to be a actor ever since I was the age of eight when I was in

the school play Peter Pan of course I'd played Peter. That was the happiest day for my

mother since that was the first school activity I ever been.

There he was this fine ass motherfucker I begin to rise to the occasion in my

pants I begun to think about something else. He was walking down the aisle I quickly

walked straight past him tying my best to avid him with all my might. Beside I was going

though a recession I didn't need a man as fine as he is detracting me from my true

passion which was acting so I thought at the time. Every now and then looked up at him

just to catch a glance of his fineness. This went on for about six months till he came to

me needing some type of help. Out of all the bitches in this class I figure the nigga was

straight little did I know this thug was feenin for some of Boe. "You want me to help

you?"

"Yeah, a nigga got a better chance of passing this class. I'll even shoot you

some money." He says in a seductive tone.

I can't help this nigga out I might try get a taste some of the wood then he

had to fuck me up big time. I wasn't having that shit after I had dealt with so many beating when I was Keith. So I did what I know best or at least try my best to say no.

"I'm sorry I can't do that I have a busy work schedule and there no way I could help you."
Knowing fucking well that I don't work in fact I hadn't worked since I hook into a twisted
relationship with Kieth. He made my ass quit after the second month of dating way
before he turn into the Hell Raiser the personalty I came to deal with. He made me his
trophy wife in my mind I was prisoner. I always had to check in when I was with him
which I hated more than anything I ever had to do.

He was on some new shit shit I dealt with in my previous attempt from a guy
trying get some play even though I only been with one other person. This motherfucker is
too arrogant for me. He cleared his throat. "I can work around your schedule it don't
matter what time is. So what ya think about that?"

My bitch ass got lost in his damn eyes which was a first for me. Still tryina
another way to tell his ass no but was running lies. "Why don't you ask another
classmate in our class."

"You are the best so I gotta have the best and that's you."

I couldn't help myself I blushed like hell. He knew without a doubt he had me.
"For real I don't think I'm all that." Another lie. Damn him. Damn me. Fuck this I broke
just like that. "Maybe I could try and see if I could try to give you a shoot but this wont
be easy I plan to work you to the bone." Not paying any type of attention to the way I've
been speaking.

Two weeks later...

"I can't take you lying to me all the fucking time." I yelled to the top of my lung not giving fuck who heard me as my eyes begin to swell up.

"I'm not lying baby." He pleaded with me as he took his left researching for my left hand but snitch it away.

"Don't fucking touch me you motherfucker. I can tell when your lying to me. You always around the room. I can smell a lie twenty miles away. I told you too many times don't got dammit lie to me. You know what it's over so get your shit and get the fuck out my place." I said as I walked as fast as I could toward the front door of my apartment but my body swug around to face him.

"This the part where we suppose to kiss." He says in almost joky tone which made me blush just a bit.

"Look I know your straight from jump street so you don't have to do this but if you end up with a role something like this they aspect for you to play the part." I said in a way that my hoping he'll let me go.

The way his arm was holding me made my knees buckled. His skin smelled so freaking good and it was turning me the hell on. I gotta get out of his grip fast but frozen as if sub zero froze me himself. My lips were stuck close my eyes still glued to his.

His face lean in so close to me that our nose touched. This can't be real. Somebody slap the shit out wake me up from fantasy. Like right now do it. His lips touch mine I just melt like cheese on a burger. Sliding his tongue in my mouth. This nigga is a pro no doubt I thought to myself. He begin to use his tongue as if he was searching for mine. Our tongue begun a dance of there own. Then he finally broke the kiss of death.

"How was that?" He said though a hard breath.

I wanted to tell this brother it was all that and then some. My dirty thoughts wonder how the dick game would be like in the room. Finally being able to move I removed arms from around me. Then respond. "It was alright. But it's get late."

I glance at watch it was two thirty in the morning. From the look in his eyes he didn't want to leave but ask me if I give a fuck. He ain't had to go home but he had to go some place. Shit I need my cold shower like now cause I was too turn on right now.

"What you saying B?"

Was he slow or something. I sucked my teeth. "What ya think meant? It's time to bounce fool that what I mean by that."

"What if I don't wanna leave just yet?"

"It ain't bout ya wanna. Time to be step on out my door." I said with a slight attitude. I ain't bout to front I didn't want him to just yet but hey this brother is straight.

"I wanna work a little more on the script. I'm up for this role and wanna be ready." He told his little white lie.

"I'm totally beat from my shrift tonight. So you need to gets the stepping. Now bounce." I said while pretending to be tired.

I having a Vivian Green moment you know gotta go gotta leave so please don't it hard for me cause he making this hard like some hard candy. This dude getting to me in the worse way.

"Well I'll leave since you throwing a nigga out. See you in class tomorrow." He started talking like a little boy which made me feel somewhat bad.

"Alright later."

He turns towards the door to leave I was right behind him closely. When he reached the front door he quickly slammed it shut. I begin to be afraid of him instantly. He must've saw though my expression cause he pulled me into his arms as I tried my best to push away from him but my lips landed on his.

I was both scared and yawned for him at the same time that my body went all direction. My mind got confused on it's instructions. Not him he knew just what to do. Finally it hit me this dark skin nigga wanted me for a while and here I am thinking he was straight. Shit he straight up wanted to fuck the living shit out me.

I refuse to go down like that. A vision to Kieth came into mind then forcing me to use all my muscles moving myself out of his intense embrace taking about ten step away form him. "I came do this."

"What you mean? You started it." He said looking puzzled as can be.

"No I didn't and you know that. You just need to leave for real." I insisted folding my arms loosely to my chest not really sure what I wanted to do with them.

"Okay, I like you, Brandon."

"I thought you were straight. You came in miss represent yourself. And just so you know I ain't easy by a long shot." I narrow my eyes at him.

"What makes you think something was going down this morning?" He give make this weird expression as if he was trying to figure me out but before I could speak a word he continue on. "I had my eyes on you for a while. A nigga didn't know how to

come at you. So I pretend I had needed help with my acting. Can you blame me for tryina get at you?"

I thought for about it for like a moment or less bout his question. Hey I sexy like a motherfucker. These big juicy lips of mine which I knew to sure drive a trade crazy as hell.

"Look, it's getting later by the minute. I just got out of a real painful relationship that lasted for almost two years." I cleared my throat then continue on before he speak another word. "I don't expect you to be around til I'm ready to jump into another."

"I'll wait. There's something special about you. Can we be friends til then?" He said sincerely.

"That would be just fine." I yawn covering my mouth. "It's getting late for real. I'll call you or you could call me."

With that left being said good night of course. The rest of that morning I couldn't get a wink of sleep for the simple fact he was running though my mind. So to keep me from thinking bout the brother I put up a book from my favorite author **E. Lynn Harris**.

Later that I avoided him in class. Afterward I rush as fast as I could to get away from him so I wouldn't be able to deal with him at that moment. But he did called me around ten that night. We talked for seem like days. He told me he had to handle some business out of town for bout a week or less. I missed him so much that when he *surprised me at my front I was unable to hide my smile he knew he got me and that's*

how I met my man aka baby daddy bka my all meaning Khalid Hisham Steele.

Since I moved from Atlanta to Alabama about a month later the inccident

with Keith. I deided not to contact April nor Dashawn ever, you know shit happens. I

thought I could trust them but you know I thought like my momma use to say you

thought like Nelly, she thought shit was jelly. In deed I knew they had done moved back

to Savannah. Dashawn fucked ass ended up being ass out just as I expected his bitch ass

to be since that bitch used my ass by living off of me for free then had the nerve to be

going around popping that fucking mouth of his and making me the butt of his jokes,

look who had the last laugh? Ha ha, yeah baby it was me. April on the other hand hope

she wasn't doing what she use to do to get by. She was good friend except the fact she

was too noisy for her own good. The only person real that I stayed in communication

with was my college friend Asia Grey.

I laid in my bed thinking baby when the phone ranged awaken me from my

train of thought. It predicted that it was Khalid since I knew he were on the road instead

I my girl Asia. I exhaled wearing a slight attitude expression on my face. "What's up

Asia?"

"Hi Boe, how everything going with you and that new boo your hiding?" She

said sounding sad tone.

"Everything is everything with my Khalid I mean Hisham. This man must've

been sent from Heaven the god above has truly bless me with this one. I mean after dealing with a man like him it feels good to have a good one around you know." I said as my bubbled as if butterfly were flying all around in it.

"That's good B. I'm truly happy for you." Asia said still she sounded sad.

I couldn't help myself the only way I was going to get any information bout whats bothering her was to ask her so I did. "Asia the hell is going on with cause I know something wrong with you?"

"Nothing wrong with me." She said I knew she was obviously lying me.

"Why your lying to me. And don't think for one minute that a phone stop me from figure you out."

"I'm totally fine so stop tripping with me."

that did it I knew that mean she need a friend true friend and that was me. "I'm on my way." I said then hung up in her face cause had enough of the lying. I grabbed my laptop schedule a flight to Santa Monica.

My baby took me the airport he wanted to tag along but I insisted him stay and that I'll call him as soon as the plane landed. After a good passionate kiss goodbye I was off on my journey. While I was on the plane I ride I began to miss him already. My bitch ass is strung and didn't even get the dick. I told him when it's the right time for us that's when we would make love.

I made it safe and sound to Asia apartment without trouble. When she finally answer the door I knew she'd been through hell for a while from the bags under her eye. "You didn't have to come all this way Boe. I'm alright." She said coldly.

"No your not my friend so why don't you cut the bull shit and tell me what the deal." I said walking past her even though she hadn't invited me.

"Boe, I need help and you ain't able to that. Can you?" She said wearing attitude I couldn't register yet where the hell it coming from.

I dropped my shit where I were standing then place hands on my hip. Now it was me who had a fucking attitude. I didn't give a damn if she saw it either. "Depends."

"I need money?"

"For what?" I asked being noisy.

"Personal. Boe, stop being noisy and shit."

"Don't you got a Pro NFL player to ask for shit like that."

"Don't worry bout his pussy ass. See I knew you couldn't help me." She rolled her eyes.

"See that's where your wrong sweetie. I've got plenty of money. I'm here to help you cause it obviously you need me and I need you. Your my closest friend. You the only person other than that pussy ass nigga Manuel knew I was going though in Atl with Kieth. You believed me. This is my time to be there for you like you were for me." I said as I walked towards her till I stop two inches from her face to face we stood in silence for a few minutes then I spoke again. "You don't have to tell me right now but when your ready I'm here. Asia, deep down you wanna tell me anyway." I watched tears steamed down her cheeks I pulled her in my arms to embracing her because she needs it. Whatever was bothering or hurting her to the core I knew exactly how that feels. This made our friendship stronger than the one I shared with my two best friends back home meaning April and Dashawn who I known since a very young age.

Two months later...

Even though I stay with Asia for about three weeks. Khalid even came out visit me a week than headed back. Us three had a ball well at least my baby and I had enjoy our self. Asia on the other hand seen dark in another world. I noticed that bitch ass Manuel hadn't call once which pissed me the fuck off. Ugh men. What the hell I'm thinking I'm one of them. By the end of my trip she seen to come back to earth. Shit E.T phone this bitch home I thought to myself.

Khalid took me to the beach for a day about us he tells me. We did lots fun things on that beach that day. I knew he could tell I was completely happy from look in his beautiful eyes. As we laid on a beach towel I fall into a deep thought he notice. "Peanut butter, what you thinking bout?"

"Hisham, just thinking you and me. I love it here so much that I'd live on or near. It just to peaceful."

"I'll be right there with you."

"Word boo." I replied wearing a big smile. "I want us to be perfectly honest with each other. I can you do that?"

"Yeah Peanut butter. I see us together for a long time."

"You is my second relationship." I paused for a few seconds. "Kieth was the worse experience of my life." I sat up still looking in his eyes as I reveal my first deep dark secret I've kept to myself. "He cheated on me with every sissy he could find and I tried to leave but he'll beat the living she out of me than told me 'he'll kill me and put my body somewhere so no one would ever find me." I said tears began to form in my left eye.

He gazed at me with a unreadable expression as he'd listen to my sob story without saying a word. He waited patiently til I was finish then asked. "How did you getaway from that motherfucker?"

I remain quiet for a voice came out of nowhere the sparkle I once had in my beautiful eyes change. I think he saw it but didn't say a word. Then I finally spoke the sound within it still felt different. "I fought for my life that's how I did it. I made a mistake I let that bastard live to see another day. Now he'll be back to finish what I started."

"You don't look like you been though some shit like that babe. When that nigga comes back in the picture we're be ready for that nigga." He says in a cocky tone.

I cracked a smiled then replied. "How can you be so sure?"

"Marry me then I'll tell you how. Trust me once your last name change everything will for you. So what you think?" He said flashing that beautiful teeth of his.

Mix emotion about gay marriage. Marriage is a wonderful thing when your in love for a gays to jump the broom I took my hat off for them. Me on the other hand just didn't think it was for me. A few times it's cross my mind even when I was with that bastard then he knock some sense into my head. Khalid made me question everything I felt love anything in the circle of that kind of affection.

He waited for my answer wasn't sure what to say. I decided be real with man in front of me. "I don't believe in gay marriage is for me. It's cute when I see other people do that but it me."

For a minute he say a word guess thinking is what I that to myself. He leaned over towards my face. I begin to feel the hairs on the back of my neck. A feeling I knew to well came over me when he'd said in a tone I didn't recognized. "You never us like that?"

"Sometimes." I replied bluntly. Wasn't feeling tone and I let it known. We never exchange words like these but prepared to stand my ground as I raise to my feet. What the hell wrong with his ass. Shit what the deal with him I mean for real.

"What the fuck you mean sometimes?"

"What the fuck I just said? Nigga you tripping for real. Need to cool off real quick fast and in a hurry." By this time we was standing toe to toe face to face neck to neck and whatever else you can think of.

Next thing I knew he kiss me deeply. I used both of my hand to push his ass fuck away from me with anger in my eyes. "Ain't in the mood to be kissed. What you do hit me too. I been though enough pain to let you hit me cause I don't believe gay marriage." I said as tears started to fall from my eyes.

"I'll never hit and you know that deep in your heart. I want to spend the rest of my life with you when the time is right you will feel the same for me I know it." His voice soften to the knew I loved bout him.

"I love Khalid Hisham Steele. Just give me sometime I'm still tryina heal enough to give you all of me. I promise." I confess like I'm Usher Raymond singing bout his confessions.

His eyes brighten eyes reminding of a little boy getting a piece of candy at the dentist. I shock the hell out of myself. I never knew this could be like this. "And peanut butter I love you since the first time I saw you with that bad ass walk of your. You had me like D-A-M-N."

That night we made love for the first time. The dick was I mean is on point got me singing in tongues. "A baby, baby." Bout three months later we got jumped the broom. Oh wee sweetie pie. What can a motherfucker like me say but "I do" take you for the rest of my life.

About a week and half later Asia begun to feel somewhat normal. Didn't see much of Brenda and Brandon except the constant three phone calls which they had every two or three days. She pretend to be fine they started get subspecies of how she was really doing so she lied saying she busy. She was curled up on the sofa watching Marathon of Parker's when the knock at door interrupt from enjoying her peaceful afternoon she'd slowly lift herself from recliner then proceed to door. As she look through the peep hole. "Who is it?"

"Asia, I know you could see us so open this picking door." Said Brenda looking back at the peep hole as though she could see her staring back her as Brandon stood right behind her with his arms fold wearing a blink expression.

She open the door with disapproving expression on her face as she let them pass her. "Why didn't you two just didn't call before you two just show up my damn door? It good seeing you though."

"I don't give a damn what you were doing nor about you to do. You keep giving us the dis and I ain't leaving til you explain why. Before you give me a lie know I know you all to well and don't got no time for the lying mess you be throwing my way. I'm here for you and so is Brenda. We care about your stank ass. Can't figure out why we do but we do. Through thick and thin." Brandon protest concern he is. Walking into the kitchen open the refrigerator like he lived there instead of across town with his man pulling out gallon of orange juice fixing his self a drink. Return back into the living room sat down then looked back at Asia. "I waiting sweetie. Shit I can wait til next week besides Khalid and I having a disagreement."

"What happen?" She asked trying to change the subject knowing Brandon wasn't falling for it. Shaking she knew he was about to say something before he could respond to his first thought she cut him off. "Okay, okay I been feeling like shit lately. I thought it was something that disagree with my body. Guys I never felt like this this long I thought I was gone die. One minute I'm fine then the next like shit. I made appointment for Friday to see my doctor."

"How long you been feeling like this?" Brenda asked crossing her legs.

"A few weeks ago."

"You and that Manual ain't been fucking?"

"NO. We ain't did shit." She said attitude raising out of her seat.

"When was the last time you got some dick?" He matching her tone rolling his eyes. Using his left hand to remove braids off his shoulder looked at Brenda then return his attention back at Asia.

"Why you wanna know all that?"

"You on some slow shit cause just know Brenda catch my drift by now. Didn't you lady B?"

Brenda just knew she was the shit for the sample fact she was never ever been refer by any other than the name on her birth certificate. She started to blush like a school girl when nigga notice her. "I went though the same shit when I was pregnant Arnazjah."

"I just can't be. Not me what am I gonna do with a baby? Then I would be tied to that jack ass Roc forever."

"It wouldn't be that bad. Roc is a good man I think he would be a good daddy for you two baby." Brenda said trying to comfort her friend as she rubbed on her back lightly.

"Compared to that nigga Manuel he's a angel." Brandon thought for a second then added. "Who am I to judge those fools. I stay full of it. Hey? Let's make sure you got a bun in the oven."

"Come on so we can get a test from the store." Brenda says as got up from next to the sofa pulling Asia along with her. She was worry bout her friend.

They ride in Boe's BMW to the nearest store that was open. Brenda picked out the best pregnancy test she could find. Back at her crib she went into the bathroom to handle her business then return to the room find them both looking at her like she was crazy expression. "Come and sat your ass down so we can talk about your ass." Brenda said then started giggling.

"Shut up Brenda."

"So what if you is carrying one for real? I mean this changes everything between you two."Boe protested wearing a light smile.

"Shit ain't gone change cause it not gone be a baby. The test is going to come back negative. This gone be one test I'm ecstatic fail. Roc a womanizer that mean he might never change. Don't want no child of mine seeing him do a woman all kinds of way. That's the true reason I didn't want a relationship with him. Can you blame me?"

"No I don't."

"You knew what you were doing when you did the deed. So do yourself a favor and stop acting like he ain't shit cause when I wasn't here for you all the time. Something like this could make or break a nigga. He might become the man of your dreams. Asia, people do change but after having a person like my ex fear would take over who you are. Don't let fear get in your way." Brandon as he walked over on the right side of her leaning his head on her shoulder while Brenda on her left rubbing her back comfort her eyes began to get water.

"He got a point there. He got a right to know that he got a baby on the way." Brenda chime in back Brandon.

"This must be team up on Asia night. What if he say he don't want shit to with baby? Then I got to take care the baby along with myself." Asia said then wipe a tear before would fall down her cheek. Confuse she is and she didn't know for sure whether not she was caring a baby.

"Then you put his ass on child support. Asia you got me here to you. Besides you know I am a stay at home mom." Brenda murmured to Asia.

Asia imagine a life with Roc and this baby in his arms as he sang to him a nursy rhyme rocking back and forth. She laid in bed pretending to be asleep adoring the view of the perfect family she never had gowning up. Her mother was there when ever she wasn't chasing a man around while her father drink his back out.

The sound of Brandon voice bought her out of deep thought of Roc. He asked coyly. "Isn't it time for the test results?"

Asia looked at her watch then replied shaking up and down. "I don't think I could do." Looking at Brandon then Brenda then return back to Brandon. "Could you do it for me a favor Brandon? Go and read it for me."

"Why the fuck it gotta be Brandon who go read it?" Brenda without missing a beat jumping up out of her seat.

"Brenda don't be a hater all your life dammit. Hate in the morning, noon, and at night. Do you haters ever take a day off?" Brandon said then started laughing. He was too use of people throwing salt on him even though he knew Brenda wasn't nothing like that.

"I don't hate on no imitation crab. Shit you gotta have something for me to hate on." She join in on the laugh while Asia sat there with this pissed off expression on her face.

She simply rolled her eyes at the thought of them cracking jokes at a time like this. Hey this was her life they were playing with. When Brandon saw her expression he jumped rushing to the bathroom to get the test results. It took him all of three minutes then suddenly there was a flush of the toilet finally he appeared in the doorway of the bathroom shaking his head at Brenda.

"Well imitation crab what does it say?" Brenda said with a straight face. She felt like she was *Passions* waiting for the dramatic scene in the last minute that will her hanging til the following week. She hated when that happens. But here she was waiting for answer that could change her home girl life in one way or another.

Asia take both of her hands cupping her face cause she didn't want to see Brandon face cause she would know the answer without a doubt. This would change the course of her life. She felt like she wouldn't ever be a good base on her example gowning up.

"I...I... you is..." He stuttered trying his best to drag it out like he was a take show host. "Asia you..."

"Motherfucker stop that damn playing and give us the answer before I fuck you up." Asia yelled to the top of her lungs. She done had enough of the bullshit from him.

"Okay damn. I guess we can start buying baby shit then. Cause Asia you with child." Brandon said in disbelieve.

"You lying." Asia cried.

Brenda jumped not really believing Brandon mainly cause of his expression on his face. Walking over towards him then snitching it from his hand. "Oh snap Asia, he ain't playing. You got a bun in the oven alright."

Asia begin to whaling like a new born baby waiting for it's bottle. She couldn't believe the results has came back the way it did. Now she didn't know what to do. Her emotion went in all directions.

Brandon and Brenda walked over to her then embracing her. The only thing they thought might actually work oh so they thought. Brandon knew everything will be fine he had faith that she'll bounce back on her feet. She fallen before and raise back on her feet. Brenda been there when she was her little girl so knew it was a challenge she that would be worth it in the end. They sat in silence as Asia continue to cried.

"Baby, you got some good dick. I don't think I wanna leave." Candy said breathing hard as she rested her head on his chest dripped in sweat. Soft music played in the background.

"You ain't leaving no time soon, there's more to go around." Roc said feeling like he was the shit. Wearing sinister smile feeling like he is on top of the world. "Exercise me while go release myself in the bathroom."

"Baby, can you bring me a bottle water?"

"Alright." He said with his deep sexy of his as he walk out the room. When he left bathroom there was a knock at his front door. "Who is it?"

"Asia."

A voice he didn't expect to hear from no time soon. He wonder why she didn't use her spare key she has on her but was glad she decided not use for the simple fact. "Hold up I gotta put a pair of pants." He said as he rush to his bedroom. "Look Candy, a friend of mine is in the living room. I'll back in few minutes." He said then left her in the bed.

Candy climbed out of the bed her searching for something to throw on. She found a jersey at the foot of the bed. Putting it on and nothing else then she ease her way towards the bedroom door. Eavesdropping on his conversation just in case something juicy came up. She truly shock to discover his friend is a female which he didn't inform her of.

"I hope didn't catch you at a bad time being that I just showed up unannounced and all." Asia murmured.

"Yeah I got my lady in bed and she don't know nothing bout you. So what you want?" He said with a attitude.

"It could wait." She said sadly.

He sense something on her mind hoping she wasn't come over for some dick cause that spot is already taken be damn he wanted another taste of her sweet pussy he thought to himself. Man Candy done fucked him senseless. He didn't have time to be wasting. "Just tell me now. I don't have time for beating around the bush."

"No, it could wait. What you doing tomorrow round launch time?" Asia asked obviously she didn't want to discuss the matter at hand for the simple fact that he had a guest in his bed.

"I don't know but what you wanna talk about?" He asked with a attitude folding his arms tight to his chest.

Then bedroom door swung open then Candy storming in the living room with a nasty attitude to match her walk. Stopping on the side of Roc. "WHAT do you want with my fucking bitch. Cause it look like you tryina get at him if so sweetie he's taken."

"Miss, I don't know you and *you* surely don't know me so I think you need to stay in lane by minding your on business. For real. This is between Roc and I." Asia pleasantly as possible narrowing her eyes back and forth at Roc then his guest.

"Well, I'm in this so what you gone do sweetie." She said tryina inch past Roc but grabbed her arm just to keep her from going farther.

"Baby, claim down. Asia, call me what's wrong?" Roc demanded.

"You know we don't discuss personal matter in front of either of our the people we're are doing? Thought I knew you better than that. Like I said before *we* could do this at another time call me when your ready meet to talk about this." Asia said gaining control of the situation at hand as she turn to open the front door then closed it once she was out making exit out of Roc apartment.

"Who the hell was that Roc? I don't time to wipe a bitch over some dick. I didn't have time for those stupid chicken heads coming to your door this time of night." Candy protest her feeling while pointing fingers in his face.

"She just a friend that's all." He lied. She didn't need to know all the detail of his past of his relationship even he did slept with her.

She storm back into his bedroom in search of clothes. She took off Roc jersey putting on her panties and then bra. "So I suppose to believe a woman that arrive this late is just a friend."

"While it true." He partly lied.

By this time time Candy done had on her jeans and blouse on then proceed walk past grabbing her purse. Glancing from the corner of her left cutting her eyes at him. "Sure boo, whatever you tell yourself to help you sleep at night." Without another word she was gone. She wasn't she *just a friend* shit and knew better. As approached her Honda getting in she grabbed her purse finding phone searching for the second last call that was on her call log then press the call button placing it her ear. "Hello." She said when they finally answer which was on the second ring.

"You better you what have been to told." The caller murmured in a ugly tone that caused the worry lines on her forehead appeared she sucked her teeth. Before she could respond he began to speak once more. "Who the fuck you think you is sucking her goddamn teeth. I come right in your face and rearrange that motherfucker for you, bitch. Do you hear what the fuck I am saying to slut? If it wasn't for me given you this job be sucking on a trashy ass dirty ass nigga dick."

"I'm sorry boss. I won't do it again."

"Your fucking right your sorry ass bitch. Did even do what I told you to do?" He asked.

"Yea, I did what say. So what's next on our plans?" She asked rubbing her head then started the car then left from in front of Roc apartment.

She was begin to get cold feet doing something that was on blood but she need what lies on end of the deal she made the devil. Candy had some kind feeling towards Roc but what could she do confess everything which she know just yet and she was sure he'll her if she told what she know.

The downside of this was dealing with a boss that will talk to her all kinds of way. Every time she met with her he'll either threaten her or laid his hands on her which she was afraid for dear life. She knew as long as she work for him she knew she wasn't safe.

Tears begun to roll down her cheek instead of wiping them away she just let them fall. "Don't worry bout what is already in motion you just do what you doing then we both be good. He might call you when he thinks your home. Please act like your in control sometimes you don't bring your A game. And we meet in public you better act like we don't know each other."

"Okay, okay. I got you." She says with attitude rolling her eyes like he was right in her face. "I'll check in with you tomorrow. Alright?"

"Bitch, are you tryina handle me like I'm one of your John's? You better know who in control and remember every time you caught a attitude like your in control knowing full well I'm king of this shit always has been too." He yelled to the top of his lungs cause he knew without a doubt he was in control.

three days has past till Roc work up the nerve to talk with Asia who has been calling him like none stop leaving messages two to three times a day. He talked to her briefly with coldness in voice as he agreed to met up with her for lunch.

He made dinner plans Candy in a attempt to reconcile with her. He truly did missed her to the point to sending red roses to her door everyday til she return her phone call. For the life of him he couldn't figure out why she had him sprung. She stayed on his mind more than any female he dealt with before. Yet he knew he wasn't in love but he had to have her like she was the last piece of pussy.

He wear his favorite navy blue Gucci Suit and dress shoes his hair freshly cut he just knew he was the shit every time he turn his head saw some sexy ass chicks checking out his swag.

He showed up about ten minutes late just so he could piss her off. Asia a thing bout timing it was a pet tease. So he wear a smile to match how he felt. "I'm sorry I'm late hope you wasn't waiting too long." He said in a almost sympathetic smile but frankly he couldn't give a damn how she felt.

"Oh, you good I barely been here a minute so it was okay." She with a light smile as though she knew he was gonna be on purpose. "I just came from the doctor office."

"Everything went okay with that?" He asked concern in his voice. Now it was he that felt guilty bout his actions. What if she was dying or something. Roc felt guilty without a doubt in his mind but then again it could be nothing.

"It depends how you look at it." She said glancing at him the menu. She was nerves and he couldn't figure out the life of what she wanted to talk him bout.

The waitress came over her name was Lily. She place there drinks in front of them he had a cake while she just had herself a glass of orange juice. The waitress take there meal orders then she left again to give the chef they're order.

"Asia, I don't have time for the games so just tell me." He said with a slight attitude.

"It ain't easy you telling you something this personal. Roc this is a life changing. It efforts you as well me. Don't understand the situation we are in." She pleaded with him trying get where she was coming from.

"What could effort my life? Is you dying or something?" He asked wondering what really was this about.

The waitress arrived again but this time with there meals placing in front of them then neatly place her arms on her side then asked. "Is there anything else I can get for you guys?"As though she couldn't tell they were a couple or not.

Asia let her know that she was good but he on the other hand had a different approach that neither of them saw coming. He shifted in his towards the waitress direction then said with a mean ass attitude. "I think you should take my food cause I'm suddenly ain't hungry as I thought." He said then waved his meal off at her. She took the meal away without a word.

Asia had a puzzled expression on her face as she asked him. "What's wrong with you?"

"You tell me why you can't be straight with me. Woman, you of all people know I can't stand shit like that. Damn." He said with a pissed off attitude his tone in his voice that few people looked in there direction.

"That's you Roc, but I ain't and play a games with you. Shit this is so hard for me to." She said matching his attitude.

"Just tell me." He said.

"You really want me to tell you what fucking bothering me." She begin to yell not caring who was looking at her as the tears started to form in her eyes not being able to control her own body nor her emotion.

"Hell yeah I wanna know and the fuck you crying for?" He said jumping out his seat as she follow his lead.

She yelled as the tears stream down her face. "I'M THREE MONTHS PREGANT WITH YOUR FUCKING BABY."

He stood shock speechless for what seem like a minute then the words came to his. "What did say cause I think I've you say your my baby?"

Asia tremble controllable unable to keep her eye contact to man in front of her. She rolled her hard as she could at him before she speak a with a word the waitress walk back over in a hurry to settle the disagreement at hand. "Is everything okay over here cause you two are causing a scene?" She said obviously she knew what going on with a attitude placing a hand on her hip.

"Mine your fucking business." He yelled at the waitress not paying attitude he was drawing on himself at that point.

"I'm sorry for my behavior as well his. Could you please my stuff in the to go bag I'll eat it when I get home. Thank you so much." She said politely while reaching into her purse pulling out a twenty dollar bill along with her credit card handling it to the waitress. When the waitress left them then she looked back at his direction wondering why he was acting wretched with her and now with other people in public. She thought he a classy man up until this very moment. Was it cause she give him some which she known to drive a nigga crazy but this was too much for to deal with. "You need to claim down."

"I don't need to do shit. Is it mine?" He paused then added. "You been fucking with that Manual Parker properly."

"You know me better than that. I-" She said then he interrupt. Oh hell no she didn't just said that to her like she get around like that.

"I thought I knew you but a chick tend to play mind games. It just was one time now you tryina throw a child on me. I ain't going out like that." He said in the background a few men was cheering saying shit like "you ain't girl."

Waitress came back over with receipt to Asia while she was signing it the waitress simply shook her head left and right then rolled her eyes at him. When Asia handed the receipt she uttered under her breathe as as she walked away. "Men ain't shit. Can't believed he thinks after one time she can't conceive a baby."

"You know me well enough to know that I ain't been with a man in almost two years before that one night stand. Speaking of that ever since that one time your the one who been acting out like a little bitch ass hoe which you are. I tried to spare your little feeling but since you cross a line on me I'll let you in on a secret which not really not a secret." She said lean just a bite closer towards him causing effort. She could hear a few female say "tell his ass girl" and "niggas ain't shit" all over the place. "I never saw nothing but a friend. Who am I to get in a relationship with a womanizer like you you change women like you change your draws. Shit just be glad a chick like me give you some and shut your fucking mouth cause you look really like a fucking fool." She said then grabbed her things then left him with his mouth open so wide a fly could've flied in. he was dump founded and felt embarrassed for the simple fact people were looking at him like he was the fool.

Khalid was getting ready to take care some business across town. He was later planing a special dinner with Brandon to try and reconcile their relationship.

It's not that he didn't care him, It was that fact he change from the innocent masculine which he drawn to in the first place. He never could stand the feminine type. Sissy got on his nerves. Brandon carried himself like dude but hint of feminine which always not noticeable to the untrained eye.

Brandon was sitting on the sofa when his cellphone ranged startled him while he was taking loose the braids he just had put in less than two weeks before for the fact Khalid demanded for him to do so. The past few weeks they he seem to not stand the sight of me. Brandon cared a great deal for Khalid he'll do just about thing meaning dying for him.

The phone continued to ring til he got fled up and answered with a rudest attitude. "What you want cause you messing with my me time?"

"I told him and he went on excusing of having sex with Manuel. Can't believed that he done me like that in public of all the places to act a fool." Asia said crying in her car driving back home from a disappointment lunch she just had with Roc.

"Maybe Roc needs time to deal with the news bout the baby?" Brandon said not really into the conversation he was having on the phone but was into his issue.

"Maybe Roc ...needs a...attitude check for real cause his bitch ass is...getting on my fucking nerve with that dumpiness." She said through snuffles as another right tear falls from eye.

"Well, tell me how you really feel?" Brandon said sarcastically tryina cheer her up but it wasn't working. He was in one of his off days when do nothing right by nobody.

She snapped not sensing the weird vibe she was picking up on Brandon. She wasn't in the mood for his foolishness at that moment. "I don't got time for your smart ass mouth you got. I thought I could call to talk you obviously I can't do that. Good day Boe." She said then hung up with the quickness before he could even respond.

Brandon just dropped his cellphone on the side of him as if nothing has happen then went back to undoing his braids. He could feel Khalid in the behind round doing something in the room he assume that he was getting ready to handle some business someplace.

When Khalid appeared in the living room he instantly came to a halt when he notice Brandon taking out his braids. He became full of anger. "What the fuck you doing taking out those braids?"

"I guess I told myself to take them out cause that's what I'm doing Boo Boo. Khalid, I swear you *needs* to stop tryina be my god or some shit like, if you didn't know it before then you should have been catch on to the game." Brandon said as he continue to loosen his braids rolling his eyes sucking his teeth at Khalid.

Khalid power walked over to the sofa used both of his hands snitch Brandon up off the sofa looking straight in his brown eyes. Now he was pissed the hell off at the fact that he had the balls to try an handle him like a child. "I taken care of you like a man and your ass don't even work. All I ask is one thing then you start acting like a queen. If you don't have your hair the way it should be then you need to be out of here with the cloths on your back." He said releasing him from his grip then walked toward the front door when he reached it he turn the door knob then went halfway out the door. "Oh yeah. If do decide to to leave make sure you leave my money too." Then he close the door.

Later that day just before the sunset Brandon sat staring out the glass window still thinking about the argument he done had with Khalid. Once again he was startled by the sound of his cellphone on the sofa. He walked over to answer it with yet another attitude when he answer. "What you want?"

a familiar voice came over to his ear through the receiver. This person he hasn't spoken to in queit a while. "What you been up to these days?" He said with a light deep voice.

"Catching hell. It's a good thing you called me cause I was just gonna call you." He said as a smile appeared on his lips. He just knew if they put there brain together he'll show Khalid what he was all about.

"For what?" He asked in a puzzled tone. Sounding as if he was shifting his body from one side to the other.

" I don't wanna talk about this over the phone. When can you come down here?" he asked rubbing his head.

"I'll meet you in about an hour at our spot. Please don't be late cause you know I can't stand for you to be late. You know you got a neck for being late." He said in his seductive voice of his.

"I won't be best believe that."

"Okay, it you say so. I'm leaving out now." He said rolling his eyes cause he already know he'll be late as usual. He hung up in Brandon face without even saying goodbye. Looking in the eyes of his friend who was tying his shoes looking back at him. "Oh shit. You know he getting on my damn nerves can' handle at all."

His company was now standing in front of him straightening their cloths. Then he reach on the nightstand next to the phone to grabbed his Gucci Rolex. "Whatever you do count me out of it. Aight?"

"Your already in this til the end." He said lifting himself off the bed walking past his guest he begin to dress his own self. A sense of coldness came over him as he put the finishing teaches on his outfit. He mind went to a whole new level that he himself was truly ready for no doubt.

Candy was sitting on a park bench waiting Roc . He called her a little after four o'clock saying he need to speak her. She already knew the deal and how to play. Break up to make up was her plan and also her sponsor as well.

The sun was about to set which was her favorite time the day. The perfect setting to be with the one you truly love. She thought Roc is almost good ideal man of her dreams except for the floss that came with dealing with him. This dude is a compete sex addict. Sometimes she couldn't keep up with him. Meaning she couldn't take the dick but she had to let him think she could other waise she would've gotten kick to the curb which she didn't want to happen.

Finally she spotted him walking towards her from the distance with yellow roses in his left hand wearing a flat smile. She wonder what was going though his mind *anyway the wind blows I know* she thought to herself.

When he handed the roses over to her she politely taken them from him. She snuffed them putting on a fake smile pretending she'd liked them when she hated them but she loved lily more than anything in the world. "Their are lovely baby."

"My bad about last night. You forgive your man?"

"What makes you think your my man in the first place?" She pretended to be joking with him. She knew deep down that she'll might never see him as a man of her dreams but until he arrived she would simple have to deal with Roc.

His face changed into to to have a serious expression he once had earlier in the beginning of his lunch date he had with Asia before things went out if hand. He had mix feelings about Candy, Asia, and her pregnancy. He thought to himself there was possibility that baby could be his the reality has started to set in. Could he be a good father to that child or any other child he might father.

He cleared his throat looking into Candy eyes as though he was trying to hypnotize her with his own eyes. "I need to talk to you about something serious and I don't think you gonna like it. This might make or break our relationship. But I know you gotta know this so I'm just gonna spit it out. Last night I've lied but not really lie. Asia, is a friend that that part is true. A few months ago we had a night stand now she's pregnant."

Candy got up placing both of her hands on her hips. "I can't believe this shit. I don't do baby mama drama."

"Babe, Asia is nothing like that at all. We could make this work." He assured her but she wasn't buying it not one bite.

"Make her do a paternity test then maybe. Cause Candy don't do baby mama drama." She said rolling her eyes hard after folding her arms. Her perfect sunset setting gone down the drain she thought to herself.

Roc got up off the bench walk to her while her back side turned to him placing his arms around her. When she turn to face him wore a look of sadness in her eyes. He use his right hand to wipe away a tear that done touched her right eyes. He hoped that he could save his relationship with Candy, Asia on the other hand he wasn't so sure about.

Candy knew without a doubt in her mind or should she say her *boss* demand would work like a charm. He says know how to play with a nigga emotion. She thought this type of foolishness would work on a man but now she gotta take note of this mess right now.

He stood there on the deck looking out in the distance. Wearing a black Sean John with about buttons revealing his matching tank top denium jeans. The outfit wore was so glue to him like a second skin to him. No matter if you are a man or a woman you could fall under his spell.

Finally he shifted slight to the right sensing a present near him. The look on his face let Brandon know he didn't play no stupid games with anybody. Brandon of all people knew not to try him like a dog on a leash.

There eyes meet. Brandon cleared his throat. "How long have you been waiting out here?"

"Since the time I've told you to be here which was about a hour ago. I'm sick of giving you a time and you come the time you wanna show up. You been dealing with me for how long and you still can't seem to remember the time?" He asked not really wanting the answer from Brandon mouth but his ear to comprehend the words coming out of mouth. He knew how he felt about time and yet he tested him by showing up late at every meeting they had. Before Brandon a sound mouth he continue on. "What the fuck did you do to that goddamn hair? I invented way too much money into you so you fuck it up for me. I had you grow your hair out cause I told him I loved my hair long and the longer it got that's how much I loved him. We both agreed if I cut it that means I wanted the relationship to end. You just messed up my perfect relationship that we built together."

"A relationship you wasn't apart of how long?" Brandon asked then continue on how that he had the floor. He moved from side to side waving his hands all over the place. For a second you would have thought he were Dashawn or some no class ridiculous queen hitting the stage for the first time in his. He was asking to get his ass beat right there on the point. "About year now boo boo. What makes you think you he'll want you when he finds out what you been up to? Bitch, he ain't gone want you. I thought I needed your help but I'm good Boo boo." Brandon turned walking away suddenly I snitched by his left arm which spinning his body around back around to face guest.

"First of all I ain't nobody bitch. Your ass must've been around that hoe way too long. Second of all Khalid always been mine just because he give you some dick every now and then don't mean a motherfucking thing to me. Plus that shit don't qualified to make you think he's your man. He like a nigga to act like he got a dick between his legs not a pussy cause that's what see you acting like. I train you to be a class A in discreet and classy not trashy. You can be on your way now cause your fucking this up for me. The money is in the bank account I made in your name I got it from here. Puff be gone."

He said as he walked past him stepping on his ego which got bruised by the sucker punch.

"Ya really a piece of work." He said placing both of his hands on his hips the rolling eyes hard. He was truly pissed off at the situation.

"Yea, that's why my name is Brandon Omar Edwards. The baddest thing that walked the street ever. You should have known that lil boi." I said then walked away with victory in my step. I know the tale just got real. I could turn a romance dream into your worst nightmare in the hood. All good this thing come earthquake in some point in our lives. Unfortunately the tale of my life is what it is in my world. Your ass needs to catch up with the quickness.

When I stepped up in Khalid house on the hill I just knew this bitch put all this foolishness in my man's castle. This is a reason why he never been here the way he use to be home on the regular. I walked completely around the house in disguising attitude cause of the bull shit so call decoration all over the place. The first thing I touch was this big motherfucking photo of the so called queen version of myself over the fireplace walking it over the hallway then went back taking down other doing the same thing over and over till of the picture were all off the living room wall. Entering the kitchen I could hear the front door open then close. I didn't even bother ask who was there cause I already knew the answer to my question. Instead I grab this bullshit after bullshit into trash can which was the only thing I liked in the kitchen, my reason is cause I brought the sucker. When I got finish the kitchen was nearly empty.

"What the fuck in the hell did you do in here?" Khalid yelled at me like he was out of his mind by the time I done a about face my eyes meet his the only thing I saw was complete anger in my man's spirit. At first I didn't have a responds for him. This is some new shit I thought to myself while I used one of my hands to play with my hair. I continue to let him be a man you know let him be in control of the situation or at least let his chocolate ass think he was in control of me. When I was ready to make my move trust I was gonna do it real fast. I must say my man sure do need how to look sexy mad. Damn. His jawline how they clinched they do. He never seen him this way guess that what happens when you let a *queen* do a pro job. Finally he got tired of all the arguing he been doing leaving the room looking frustrated. He did that this shit on me.

When the time I made my entrance into the bedroom I almost throw up. The room was decorated in red, black, and green from the curtain to the rug. This bitch just fucked up my man's throne. Don't worry king B is here to make everything all better. I could hear the sound of rain coming from the bathroom. So I knew that Khalid was in the shower.

I begun to undo my sheet dropping it on the floor then kicking off my new pair of timberland boots I just brought yesterday then continue taking off the rest of my clothes till I was done with them all off my slim sexy body. My hair was all over the place at this point. This would be the first time in a while I wouldn't mess with it. I turning the knob cracking the door sneaking a view of my baby through the steamy room. Damn this chocolate almond got it going on. I know he got plenty of nut building up in those balls just for me. I ease myself into the bathroom. He didn't seem to notice me in front of him just checking out his big juicy phat how hung sausage between his legs for the simple fact his eyes where closed. I wanted to rock his nerves. I position myself on my knees while inching my lips towards the head of his dick catching it without any hands but with my mouth. He tried to yanked me off of his dick. You know I held my ground as I sucked on that motherfucker like I were a vacuum machine on that monster. He couldn't help himself by using the wall to hold his balance. Bringing my lips away from the microphone to see that bad boy standing rock hard for me. I then kiss the side of his leg leaving a trails up towards his face til we standing face to face. He was breathing hard trying to caught his breathe.

"What the fuck you trying." He said still trying his best to push me away from him. He was in for fight for his life.

"Daddy, what's wrong? I thought you love when I talk to the mac?" I asked with flirtation in my voice looking into his eyes with my saddest puppy dog expression I could make.

"What?" He asked confused.

"What ain't what said. Baby, you been playing these game so long that you can't recognize the real me. That queen sure did a number on my husband. Calm down and let your better half make it all better." I knew I jumped out of character one of the few times I ever done. You properly second time get surprise by the dirty lil Boe but your ass needs to catch up with a playa.

"What your doing here? I thought we were gonna do this for another year then fire that motherfucker for good this time." He said with a concern in his eyes looking back in my eyes.

"You of all people should know how plans could change at any given minute. Baby, just chill it just was time for us to stop hidden our relationship. The ain't gonna show up cause there no trances to leave them back to me." I said reassuring Khalid that everything gonna be alright. They had to be.

He wasn't sure even there to do the actual act in the crime that part was all on me and I did that part real well I must say myself. No matter what I got his back and I know he got mine without a doubt in my mind.

The next day..

Candy walked along the pathway in the park. As her hair brushed her shoulders with each step she took she wonder why Roc wanted to met her in a public area like this. She hoped with all her might that he brought her to a place to breakup with her. She thought she was too fine to get dumped like this. She wear a pink and white sundress with matching stilettos. From a distance she could see he him standing under a cabana looking like he was weighting something heavy on him which made her feared for the worse.

She was about ten feet away when he realize that she was approaching him. He made a fake smile appeared across his face as if he was happy to see her. When she got within arm reach they embrace each other while tonguing each other down passionately. He pulled away sizing her up and down. "I was thinking bout doing that all day. Candy, I can't stop thinking bout."

She felt relieved that Roc was still under her spell for what she could tell. Still she knew something is on his mind. Dump fifth grader could tell this man is going though the emotion. She wonder if the argument from the other day was a little too much. Even though she could careless bout some other chick. Instead asking him she just assumed that he wanted to break up with her. "For real? Being that I caused a scene last night I thought you wanted to break up with me. I'm truly sorry for my action. I completely jump to the wrong concussion. I understand if you need to take a break." She said wiping a tear which done began to fume in her left eye.

"That depends on how you take what I'm about to tell you." He paused then begun to tell her of the story about him and Asia. Candy expression changed worry into a puzzle look. "Anyway yesterday she told me she's pregnant. I'll understand if you don't want no dealing with me."

Candy sucked her teeth the words of her secretive employer *no matter what it takes you better not fuck this up for* echo in her ears she knew what she had to do. She searched mind for a way to save her so call of a relationship she shared with Roc . Clearing her throat placing her left hand cross her heart acting as if she was anger. Truth be told she could have cared lose bout his situation she had to stay with him for as long as her employer said so. "Sweets, I highly doubt that your baby. A female like Asia or what ever her name is, is after one thing and that's your money. She see you done moved on now she wants you back so she used a baby to trap you. Don't be a pawn in her web of trickery. As for me I ain't going anywhere."

"I don't think it's either which is what I told her yesterday. It didn't mean a thing to me, before we even started dating." He said. He felt Manuel Parker done slept with her then left her when he'd learn bout her pregnancy then split now he was left.

"Well then there is no need for to discuss any farther. So what are you doing tonight?" She asked changing the subject. She walked to him placing her arms around his waist as she laid her on his right shoulder. Without a doubt in her mind she knew she had Roc right in the palm of her hands. It was too bad for this Asia cause she only had him once but she got him all the time.

I awake the next morning with Khalid's arms around me holding me tightly. The feel of him never felt better on my skin. I could just stay like this all day and I'll never get bored. So I just snuggle closer to his body as he begin to wake himself up. I rotate my body in the direction of his face. His eyes half open. "Good morning Hisham."

"Yes this is a *good* morning now that your here with me. How you slept?"

"*Good* like a naughty lil angel in waiting for his king to pinch to tell me I'm not dreaming." I admitted in my sleepy. He had me feeling like my ass was on cloud nine, a place in which I knew so well. He kissed me passionately on my hungry lips our lips play a game of tongue dance barely leaving any room for air to get in. He then used his tongue to trailing down my neck leading my right nipple. Awe, shit this nigga knows how to use his lips I thought to myself. The ringing of my cell phone interrupt us briefly as usual I annoyed it. Khalid comes first everybody else just have to wait. Whoever have a problem well that's they're problem. I quickly took his head pushing back toward my nipple. "Fuck whoever that motherfucker was it's bout me right now."

He lifted his head briefly meeting my eyes. "Let's just hope that ain't anybody important." Then he back down to handling his business leaving my nipples trailing on the line of my abs. It wasn't til he to my thigh when my cellphone rang again. Between nibbles he spoke. "Get it."

I made a face than reached over to answer. "What you want." I said in a unpleasant tone. Wasn't in the mood for any drama today.

"Boe, I need you to come over like yesterday. Have a emergency. Roc talking that cash money shit bout he ain't the father of our baby. He's on that bullshit. We gotta come up with a way for him to see that I ain't lying about the baby." She confessed.

Khalid kinda of made it difficult for me to listen to what Asia was saying. I tried my best not let her know what I was doing on my end. My man ain't the type to be sucking on a nigga dick so I knew what where he made use of those lips and that damn tongue of his. *And where he use it at you ask? My boy pussy baby.* "Hmm, I won't be free til later this afternoon. Khalid took me out of town on a last minute thang. We won't be back until later on in the afternoon. Is seven good?" I was lying through my teeth. My baby continue to handle his business as he entered my body. One hand on the cellphone with the other grabbed behind his head. My body is completely about to burn up.

"Know good and well what your doing cause I could hear your moans on the low. Manuel wanted to meet up for lunch. Wasn't in the mood to deal with him right now. Ever since I found out bout this baby, didn't feel like dealing with him. If he know I'm pregnant he gonna leave again." She confessed.

"As much as I don't like Manuel Parker, he ain't gonna pull that bullshit like that he did last time. That fool don't got fame no more, other than those groupie that tries to get at him from what I saw that day at the park he saw straight though with them. Asia please." I said rolling my eyes at fact what I'm saying something good bout that motherfucker.

"You think so?"

"No. I think so." I said playfully. "Look here Asia as much as I love you I love my man a tab bite more so I gotta go take care of him. Later." I hung up without even waiting for her comment. Looking back down at Khalid wearing a priceless smile. "Stop playing with that tongue need that dick like right now." I swear my body should be real swore but it's not. Instead it's repeatedly calling out for Khalid name over and over again.

Just like I suspected Manuel Parker accepted her with the baby in her belly. I encourage her to move on with her life. It didn't even matter the fact that she was moving on with Manuel as the sub. On February tenth at two thirty in the morning she had her first bundle of joy. Weighing at about eight lbs two oz. She name her Daisha

Nelson Grey but before her name could be printed on her birth certificate Manuel said that he wanted her to have his last name.

"Oh, so I'm the only suppose to be Grey?" She said rolling her eyes at him then looking at back beauitful daughter.

"That why your gonna marry me. Aren't ya?" Then he kissed her on the forehead. That was about sixteen months and half ago.

The planning time for the wedding may have been cut short but this is by far the second best wedding I have been to. The first was mine. I didn't go to April's wedding because I didn't feel like that foolishness. I mean you gonna married a man knowing that he left you for a man. That couldn't have been me that's all I'm going to say bout. No shade here.

Just a few hours before the wedding Roc Blackwell got mystery knock on his front door. When he open the door the delivery girl stand with a package in her hand. "Are you Mr. Blackwell?"

"Yes I am but I'm not expecting anything." He said with a puzzle look on her fac   "Sometimes it be that way." She said in a up beat tone after she handed him the package she held in right hand then disappeared.

Once he closed the door he notice there wasn't a return address. When he open the envelope to find a few sheets of paper the first was a note saying *here some information about your girl. The hoe would do anything for money and that includes fucking the living shit out of you. Yea, what bitch you done mind fucked? Yea, it's me* naive Lakia Wiggins. *The one who know you the best. Oh yea, I left you some more information you might wanna know bout. When you see a bitch on the street holla at her.* Anger aroused within him.

He couldn't control his self as he flipped through the pages he saw photo of himself at a party. He was naked with a woman at first he didn't recognize was Candi. This is one of those moments think he wish to remember but he does. Like it was yesterday. This was a party where any and everybody could sexed whoever they wanted which he was doing and doing it well. He never had a clue that Ebony knew about him going to these adult parties.

The last page was a paternity test of Asia Gray and Manuel Parker. To his surpraise Manuel wasn't the father so he knew that he was the father. He felt completly studpid for the way he treated her. That way last chance to get her. He'd quickly graped his cellphone dailing Asia number but she didn't answer. The next number he dailed was Candi but her cell was suddenly disconnected when it just on nomore than an hour ago. He called me but I refused to answer his call.

I was standing behind one of my down to earth best friends which I never told April and Dashawn about and her name is Asia Gray. The secret I keep on a regular day to day basis. As I tried my best to help her fix her captivating gown while she stare at herself in the mirror with a priceless smile on her face. "I can't believe your getting married. I thought it would've been a few years ago though but like the old saying better late than never." I murmured wearing a smile. "I remember Khalid and my wedding nine years and half ago. The blessing god have given him and I don't deserve it at all." Okay I can't believe I just said that bullshit aloud true is I believe in god but after what I done back in Savannah Georgia let just say if you knew me back then your think of me in a different form of light.

"Me either this day has taken me so long for us to get here but we're here and I'm glad this day has arrived." She said proudly then her mind went somewhere she didn't expected.

"What wrong? Your looking depressed." Her friend Brenda Lawrence asked while checking her make up.

"Why you think that?" Asia said shaking off her feeling.

"Brenda, I see where you going with this so please don't go there in here of all days. Even I could see what's really on her mind but I don't want to pressure her about her feeling." I said rolling my eyes at her. I been around that queen Dashawn way too long, I don't even do this rolling eyes foolishness. More time will wash away the habits which he passed upon me.

"Okay, okay, okay this is my day so you two could save it til your not in the same room with me." Asia shouted with anger in her eyes carrying a pleasant tone in her voice.

I simply shook my head wearing a smile on my face cause I didn't even feel like talking about it on her beautiful day. Brenda had a shock expression on her face I knew good and well what was on her mind but she good people so I don't blame her reason why. Before she had the chance to respond there was a sudden knock on the door. I looked Brenda then at Asia when she said "Come in." When the door open a tall dark handsome brother stepped in.

"Hey, long time no see."

"Why yes it has been. I'm glad you came it means a lot to me."

"Can we talk for just a moment Brenda and Boe." Roc asked us and we just looked at her for her answer.

"No" Brenda and I replied in unison. I was wearing the hell out of this suit. Ain't no nigga was about to make me wear this fly gear for no wedding at all. Somebody was about to get married this day, right here.

"Yo Boe, I ain't here to start no BS. All I wanna do is talk that's it."

For a almost thirty seconds there was silents among the four of us. "Just two minutes that's all your gonna get. You guys, could you give us two minute." Asia said standing her ground placing her hands on her hips. Brenda and I give him an evil eye the whole time as we marched out of the room.

Brenda and I left Asia and her unexpected guest in the alone while we converse about current events and such. "I just can't believe that fool bought his tired aspirin up in here." Brenda said with a disgusting on her face.

"You need to give give him a break that has one last chance to get her back before she jumps the broom. I mean you would understand if the shoe was on the other foot."

"*Hell* naw never in my lifetime, if so please slap the hell the out of me for doin that stupid shit. Ugh."

"I thought I was hell best you got me bet." I giggled looking at Brenda like she lost her mind. Instantly my mind wondered to Jermaine who was rumored to been married Kelly who deserved a better man. I felt like a fool for thinking he could change but like saying leopard can't change it's spots.

"Shit you number one Asia before me shit that's why we get along we each other so perfectly well. Shit I was just about to fuck you one." Brenda said then sip her drink while I on the other hand carried a devilish smile thinking of all the bull shit I've done the past and believe I've done some off the chain.

"Fish keep playing with me. Sometimes I think you wish you've lived like do now if so you can't handle what I do on day to day basis. And one more thing please stop profanity in this church."

"Oh snap this wine has got me buzzed my bad but never that. Don't play with me imitation crab meat. I just with I had a man with money so I'll be set for life." She as put her drink to take another sip of drink.

I let the words escaped my lips before I could try to stop them from hitting the air. "Be care what you wish for cause you don't know what it takes to keep him." My nerves begin to bother me something it hadn't since the night of my graduation when I break up with Kieth the way we didn't see coming but I knew it would happen something like that.

"What you mean?" Brenda question brought me back to the situation I put myself in.

"Nothing child I didn't mean a thing by that but just be careful about whatcha want." I said hoping she'll buy my little white lie.

"You never told me how you forgive him for his indiscretion a few years ago. I don't know if I can handle my man cheated on me." She said with her eyes directly at me waiting my response.

With a shock expression my face I said. "Child, what your talking about?"

"You told me that he cheated on you."

"Sh... I mean sweetie he never cheated on me." I said tryina figure out why she think that cause I would tell her if he did. I know Khalid from head to toe inside out.

"Stop playing you told me out your own mouth that he cheated own you but you couldn't prove it." Brenda claim.

"Must be somebody that look like me." I said wondering how we got on this subject in the first place but she kept on being noisy so I decided to let my eyes roam the room. A familiar face caught my attention she was standing in the far doorway but not too noticeable but she was giving me a mean mug so I did what do block her out of my circle so I get back in this conversation with Brenda which was still dead set on talking about a time Khalid allegedly had some kind of affair on me. I did my best to switch this in another direction and fast. So I used my left hand to playful twirl some of my hair wearing my condescending smile. "Oh... child ain't nobody got time to be thinking bout that foolishness your trying to disguise. All you need to know right now is that your alleged momery is playing with your mind. You might wanna slow down on the drinks before the wedding." Returning my eyes back to the far door but she had done disappear for the moment and I was glad for that.

Brenda seem like she catch my drift cause she change the subject with the quickness. "How long did you think he needed to chat with and do you still the wedding is on?"

I didn't know for sure but when it came to having two different men both with big pocket I knew she had a win win situation I was proud to her my girl. "I don't know but I hate to waste sexy outfit on a day full of promises." I blurted out while I was speaking text message came through on my cell.

"Mr. Steele meet in the hallway asap. We have business to disguise and I feel like this should be face to face."

I couldn't do a thing but blushing uncontrollably as heat starts to rise. My true emotion hasn't yet to show up on my face. Brenda looked at me like it was Khalid was texted me but it wasn't. "Sorry Brenda I make a important phone call." I murmured as I begin to stand to my feet then headed toward the before she could say a word to me. As I entered through the doubled door I could see the same female who was mean mug me like she lost her picking mind maybe she did. "So do I know you and how you got my number Ms.?"

"I know you like to role play personally I don't give-" She spit at me but I cut her off before she'd use profanity in the church.

"Ms. your the one tryina role play on me cause I don't know or have a clue to what you are yapping. Please don't make me repeat my first statement." I demanded.

"Where is it Mr. Steele?" She said annoying my question.

"I make have to take the foolishness outside cause your pissing me off. And where is what your talking about?" I said with a puzzle look on my face.

"My package you promise me." She raising her voice a tap bite no one still couldn't hear her at this point.

"What package? We know let take this outside for real."

"NO you need to let me know when you plan to hand my package over." She demanded.

"Huh, child I don't know what ya talking bout. I don't know shi... I mean nothing bout what your talking about." I said turning my back to her heading towards to the nearest exit which wasn't nothing but less than ten feet away she follow behind me closely.

"Mr. Steele stop playing where is it?" She said once they were outside and I'd stop walking a few feet outside of the church before I could turn around to face her by then my whole demeanor change in my face especially in my eyes.

When I finally turn around to face her I almost lost complete. "Darling, I think it's time for you to leave like now before I say something that might hurt your feeling."

She didn't blink as she press her lips together. "You could never hurt my feeling Mr. Steele. Should march in there and everybody your little secret. Trust me I'll do it."

"Bitch, I'll fuck you up if you try and fuck with me and my mines. I got what you want so go on make this a day to remember for the rest of your life and you don't wanna live with regret do you sweetie?" I said wearing a devilish smile folding my loosely arms to my chest. She immediately walked away without saying a word as tears fall from her eyes. As she went one way I walked back into the building dropping my arm to my side I didn't stop til I reached the restroom splashing a little water in my face.

"Having fun too much fun I see." A familiar voice said says to me while my eyes were closed coming out a stile right behind me. This day ain't gone get any better I thought to myself grabbing a paper towel drying my face.

I replied. "How so?" Not even looking in their direction while I was still drying off my face. I was begin to think this day wasn't going to get better but instead interesting by the minute.

"I want my man back." He says placing left hand on his hip starring at me but I couldn't see him cause my back was to him and I was drying my face.

"You may have had him once but I got him all the time dear. I paid you to do a job and that's all it was a J-O-B. I knew you were a weak chick and what do weak chicks do fall so easily on the job. Don't get it twisted he was never yours but he was and still is my man. You better get my left overs cause this is my man and plan to keep it that was till the day one of us die." I said using right hand to play in my hair showing off my Gucci watch slowly turning around to face him putting on my devilish smile back on forgetting I was in a church.

"I hate you. Always got to have it your way like your at McDonald's or something this gonna end today on my terms." He says trying to handle me like this way the streets or something.

"Oh really, you think you got me beat? Well we need to tell him everything and let him decide what he wants." I said looking at the other person. "You should have took the money I give you and run to start your new life."

"Khalid is my life. I love him with all my heart more than you could ever."

I said nothing for a minute the wedding was on the top of my list then this girl came up now I have this situation all in one day something had to give. This time I just might not win this battle. I knew what I sign up for the day I decided to leave Kieth the way I did. I plan on living to the fullest ride or die. I open my mouth to speak before a word came out he slap me so hard that he could have been hear halfway down the hall. I murmured a sentences strong so it rocked his nerves. "The mirror may look like me wear my clothes and even sleep with my man a little bite of the time. Don't mean you could ever be me. There is and always will be only one Brandon Omar Edwards-Steele and that motherfucker ain't no weak bitch like you. Matter of fact you even hit like a bitch. But I'll text you the time for us to handle this later." It felt like I didn't feel a single thing at all turn my face back towards the man looking identical like myself but completely like me there was marks on one our body that separating us apart.

A few years ago I was on the quest to find my father. I found him alright with a child that looked like me but he was just a little younger than me. His name is Kaan. How he got his that I could have care less. This fool follow my father hand and foot. I study their he and my father relationship. I could tell that my father was doing some fucked up shit with my half brother. This thang had some real issue. Like a year or so later the man I known as my father died suddenly.

"Where did you get that from?" Asia scream to Roc. She believe that he shown up on her wedding day. She was holding a piece of paper that he handed her.

"I'm sorry. Ain't nothing I could say to make up for how I acted. The only thing I could is move forward with our child." He said with sincere in his eyes.

She claim herself just enough to gather her thoughts. She turn her body away from him facing the mirror she begin to play like she was trying to fix her grown. With coldness in her voice. "You said what you came here to say now you can get the hell out my dressing room. Manuel is waiting on me and we must not keep him waiting."

He didn't say a word instead her left the room alone. This isn't what you expected to happen but if you know how I feel you'll be like that's what's up. The wedding was perfect no compliants from me. Most of the evening I eyes Asia to see if she was bothered by Roc visit. I see didn't see one damn thing. I send a text to my half brother of mine to meet up a little later on. I was so focus on my text that I didn't even feel Brenda walk up behind me. I was so surpraised that I almost droped my phone out of my hand. "What the hell is wrong with you?" I murmured to her.

"What ya doing playing with that phone when there is a party going on in here?" Brenda said playfully swaying her hips from side to side. Pretending like she didn't see bartender checking her out.

"Do me a favor, mind your business. Why you bothering me when there is somebody that need you a tab bite more?" I said with a half smile. To be honest I care to be bothered that much with anyone at this point my focus was on Asia.

"Who???" She asked with a curiously expression on my face.

"Your child or did you forget bout her?" I said shaking my head in disbelief. How you gone forget that you have a child? This chick have lost her mind or maybe she done had way to many drinks. Better be glad we cool. "Brenda, I'm bout to see if I could find you a ride. Somebody get you guys their safely."

"I ain't... ready to go... no where. It's just getting... started in here. And... baby girl is fine so chill." She slurred though her statment.

"Whatever, if you so happen to slip, fall, or embarressing yourself know that foolishiness is all on you." I begin to slowly walk away but not before I added. "Don't think I'm not looking for your ass a ride cause you is going home. Best believe that *sweetie pie*." If I didn't care I would've let her embarress herself.

Manual Parker was in the the center of the room dancing with the third most beatiful lady he ever laid his hazel eyes on. The first is his mother. The second is Asia the love of his life and the woman who bright the third most beatiful lady in his life Daisha. She and Asia mean everything the world to him. The sound of almost two year old Daisha Daddy non-stop which somrtimes drive Asia crazy made him smile even brighter. His smile soon fainted.

"May I cute in?" I asked nasty. I didn't give a fuck bout it being damn wedding day. Hell I wanted my god baby.

"Don't you see dancing with my lil girl?" He said with a mess up look on his face still holding Daisha.

"Really? Manuel, really? You wanna be like that, if it wasn't for me "the dealer" you wouldn't be here with a wife. Even though this is... I mean was a arrangment. So get this though that sorry ass exucuise of a brain I never approve of this. Your money the decision for me to help." While he glared at me I could tell he was pissed with me. Ask me do I care hell no I don't give a fuck. I gently took Daisha out of his hands. As Brenda came up then started dancing in front of him.

"I know you marry man, you still could dance with boo." Brenda said as she begin do a little twerk in front of him. I take that as my cue to leave the dance floor. People begin to move out of the way to see them dance. "Stop fronting like you don't wanna dance with a real woman." Manual bust out laughting as he join her with the dancing.

From the sounds of it was worthy of my time. I til I reach my maine chick. I hand over lil noodle to her mother. "Thanks Boe. I couldn't have done this without you. You a ride or die friend."

"He still think it was all his idea if he only know, you know I gotta ask ya the question is you sure bout this?" I asked.

"I could always change my mind anytime. You need to stop worrying bout me cause you know Asia, got it." She said with a smile then let out a laught so lot that people within ten feet could hear it.

I knew she made up her mind for sure with a laught like that. "Then my work has expired. Me and my king will be leaving for our second honeymoon to Hawaii. Plan on being there four about week."

"Stay in touch this time around." She said as a tear fell from her left eye. As Manual and Brenda appoach them she quickly wiped from her eye.

I walked away towards Hisham, who was waiting for me at the exit. My hubby couldn't wait any longer niether could I. You may think I did it for his money. Little did you know I got my own money plus my business before Hisham and I still got it now. This was her plan all along to get the man who left her broken in two. The same man who caused her to have a miscarriage all those years ago. True that act one has just been completed. As the reader read along they could feel my eyes on them as I took my left hand to removed a piece of hair out of my face. They were a blowed cause I left them with so many question. Guess what? You have to wait until next time Boo, Boo.

I hope u enjoy my tale of Asia Gray & Brandon Edards "Mind Games." Be on the look out for more of my love sick guilty preasure. Please be on the look out for "Imperfect Angel." which is a deeper look at me & who I am. I am who I am cuz god made me this way I am. A long this Jouney. Though the years pain he conforts me then reveal my true self. I couldn't have made it this far without him.

Printed in the USA
CPSIA information can be obtained
at www.ICGtesting.com
LVHW072147120923
758042LV00032B/268